PRAISE FOR
SURPASSING CERTAINTY

"Poignant and honest."

—*Lenny Letter*

"[Janet is] a teacher, a guide, a literary alchemist."

—*Quartz*

"Mock's gift for pairing incisive social critique with an emotionally rich accounting of her life makes reading her books a wonderful and eye-opening experience—like having a long talk with your best friend, who just happens to be a feminist trans woman of color with a rich history and a great deal to teach about how we do—and should—define womanhood. Warm and wise, *Surpassing Certainty* is a vital contribution to the growing literature on gender identity and an absorbing personal history."

—Powell's Books

"Mock breaks the shackles that have marked the 'trans memoir' genre. She is no longer offering a 101 master class on trans identity but encouraging us all to find our unique way of *being*."

—Bitch Media

"In telling her own messy, heart-wrenching, and ultimately, uplifting, affirming story, Mock has certainly set the standard—and perhaps, lit the spark of inspiration for others to write themselves into existence."

—*Bustle*

"A candid reflection on her twenties, a time of self-discovery, risk taking, and eventual success that now makes Mock one of the most visible and defining voices of trans experience."

—*Los Angeles Times*

"A beautiful, 360-degree portrait of a modern-day icon, in a way that makes it clear beyond a shadow of a doubt that [Janet Mock's] the one in charge of her narrative."

—Refinery29

"The power of Janet Mock rests in her accessibility and relatability."

—*Wear Your Voice* magazine

Also by Janet Mock

Redefining Realness

SURPASSING CERTAINTY

WHAT MY TWENTIES TAUGHT ME

JANET MOCK

ATRIA PAPERBACK

New York   London   Toronto   Sydney   New Delhi

ATRIA
PAPERBACK

An Imprint of Simon & Schuster, Inc.
1230 Avenue of the Americas
New York, NY 10020

First Atria Paperback edition May 2018

ATRIA PAPERBACK and colophon are trademarks of Simon & Schuster, Inc.

For information about special discounts for bulk purchases, please contact Simon & Schuster Special Sales at 1-866-506-1949 or business@simonandschuster.com.

The Simon & Schuster Speakers Bureau can bring authors to your live event. For more information or to book an event, contact the Simon & Schuster Speakers Bureau at 1-866-248-3049 or visit our website at www.simonspeakers.com.

Interior design by Amy Trombat

Manufactured in the United States of America

10 9 8 7 6 5 4 3 2

Library of Congress Control Number: 2017003361

ISBN 978-1-5011-4579-7
ISBN 978-1-5011-4580-3 (pbk)
ISBN 978-1-5011-4581-0 (ebook)

For the girls struggling, striving, and slaying in the shadows.
With such little light, you sparkle.
I am in awe of your brilliance.

And the speaking will get easier and easier. And you will find you have fallen in love with your own vision, which you may never have realized you had. And you will lose some friends and lovers, and realize you don't miss them. And new ones will find you and cherish you. And you will still flirt and paint your nails, dress up and party. . . . And at last you'll know with surpassing certainty that only one thing is more frightening than speaking your truth. And that is not speaking.

—AUDRE LORDE

SURPASSING CERTAINTY

INTRODUCTION

MY BACK WAS EXPOSED IN A SLINKY HALTER as I made my way through Hot Tropics nightclub, my go-to spot on Thursdays in Waikiki. It was a bit past one A.M., and the gyrating bodies on the dance floor obscured my view of someone I once knew. I recognized her face at once: wide, open, and flat, like she was pressed against a window peering in. I used to see that same face in high school, across the cafeteria. We never had a chance to say hello but we were once part of each other's every day. Oahu was small, linking locals socially by just a few steps. It was suffocating.

When our eyes met, I felt the shudder of her knowing glare. She was unmoving. I rushed for a seat in a red leather booth nearby to evade her. This also offered me reprieve from a roster of underwhelming dance partners. My bare thighs slid together as I slinked onto the seat in strappy high-heeled sandals that helped me achieve my ideal video vixen aesthetic.

Clubs are companions for those alone and awake. They fulfilled my desire to be desired and satiated my itch for a man's body against mine—close, strong, and steady. I resigned myself to the possibility of spending the night alone, because my girlfriend Cassie, with whom I had arrived, could not peel herself away from a Brazilian guy with ravenous hands. Their bodies had settled into a cozy choreography, her lean thigh lifted to his hip, his hand supporting her as she curved her back in ecstasy. Their appetite for each other seemed to mean there would be no room for me in Cassie's Lexus that night. *Good for her*, I thought, as I watched the guy pet her jet-black mane.

The drunk and jubilant revelers camouflaged me as I tried my best to recall the name of the woman from school. She was alone, tall, olive-skinned, and dark-eyed, leaning against the bar with crossed arms. She seemed unsatisfied by her own lack of prospects, which made me feel less alone. In a feminist utopia, we'd dance together, make a gleeful exit, and seek satisfaction with stacks of Denny's buttermilk pancakes. Instead, she seemed to stand in judgment.

I had long grown familiar with this particular look—knowing, intense, and direct. *She knows me*, I warned myself. In my nineteen years, I hadn't yet gotten used to the fact that nearly everywhere I went—from this club on Kuhio Avenue to the Ward Center cinemas and the pebbled walkways of my campus—someone knew me or had at least heard about me. Privacy wasn't often granted to a girl like me who had spent years standing out by merely *being*. It was the price I paid for living my truth. She knew I knew that all it'd take to shatter my fragile normality as another pretty girl in a club was a whisper. The last thing I wanted that night was for her to speak. I didn't want to be *clocked*, to be discovered, and excluded. Too many nights had ended with me upset by harsh truths that stripped me of my right to disclose and self-define on my own terms. The truth is a whip when wielded by a malicious mouth, lashing you into obedience and confinement, a stinging reminder that despite your best efforts, you are still captive to others.

I was so preoccupied by her menacing focus on me that I didn't notice the towering man with onyx skin approaching me. His full plum lips curved into a smile and made his black eyes even more narrow, like marbles in the clasped hands of a child. He looked like a model on a Sean John runway, with carved cheekbones, a square jaw, and feline eyes. His head was bald and glistening under the club's neon lights. He wore his handsomeness confidently but not cockily, commanding me to focus on him as he stretched his hand out to me.

"Can I have this dance?" he asked.

His presence left me with no other option but to peel myself from my seat. He led me to the crowded dance floor, where he spun me around and away, only to pull me back in. His hands caressed my waist, then slid to the small of my bare back. He made me feel chosen—the reason I had traded the comfort of my couch for the club. Sure, I wanted to be social, but ultimately, I wanted someone to say, *Yes, you. I want you.*

During a break between songs, I excused myself to go to the restroom.

"Can I get you a drink?" he asked.

"Ginger ale, please," I said, as I turned away with a smile.

My reflection betrayed me as I took myself in at the crowded restroom mirror. My edges were sweated out. My skin had surpassed dewy and become drenched. At least my body was snatched, I thought, despite an unceasing terror that I was just a burger away from chubbiness. I was young, and my body was resilient enough not to succumb to my late-night diet (Taco Bell Mexican pizzas, Jack in the Box egg rolls, and Zippy's chili and chicken mixed plates). I patted my face with a toilet seat liner, powdered my forehead, and reapplied a coat of MAC's Prrr lipglass before returning to the dance floor. He was standing with our drinks right where I had left him.

"I just heard the *craziest* thing." He chuckled. "You won't even believe it."

"Try me." I smiled, wrapping my hand around the cool, wet glass of soda.

"So this woman at the bar taps me on the shoulder, and I'm thinking maybe I know her," he said. "But I don't recognize her, and I just say, 'What's up?' And she's, like, 'I wasn't going to say anything, but I think it's fair that you know.' And I just nod, you know?"

I furrowed my brow in response and ripped the maraschino cherry from its stem, crunching its sweetness between my teeth. I knew where this was going. I had feared this the moment I saw her.

"And she goes, 'That girl you're dancing with isn't what she seems.' And I just look at her, because I don't know what she's talking about. So she tells me that she went to school with you and you were a dude or some shit," he said, chuckling again. "And she smiles this creepy smile, waiting for my reaction, and that's when I knew she was on some other shit. Can you believe that?"

It felt like a lash across my back, a strip of fire, stinging and burning. I didn't flinch, though. Hesitation would have served as confirmation. Instead, I cackled, doubling over as if I had just heard the most ridiculous thing *ever*. He joined me in laughter. His disbelief served as salve. He was assured that she was just a jealous girl—a hater—who wanted to push the pretty girl he was smitten with off her pedestal.

"My grandma always said that envy seeks to destroy," he said in a melodic Southern drawl that I hadn't recognized earlier. "OK, so tell me the truth," he continued. "I know you're not supposed to ask a woman this, but how old are you?"

He looked about twenty-six, so I told him I was twenty-one, lying because I was not of legal age to drink or to be in the club. I didn't care for alcohol then anyway. It made me feel out of control, uneven, slow-witted. I also didn't want to betray the trust of the doormen who let me in despite the ID I wielded. It was real, it just wasn't of me. I had bought it for sixty dollars from a friend's older cousin, a Samoan girl who was similarly hued and could pass for me with a quick scan.

"I'm Branden, by the way," he said.

"Nice to meet you. I'm Janet."

We locked eyes as if we were seeing each other for the first time, and he held my attention for a few long seconds before a familiar voice cut us off.

"Girl! Let's go to Waikiki Beach!"

It was my friend Cassie.

"Oh, sorry." She laughed in a sorry-not-sorry way. "I didn't know you were having a *moment*!"

I had met Cassie, a *hapa* beauty from Kaneohe with a taste for luxury, a few years earlier through mutual girlfriends. Initially, I hadn't cared for her, but her unabashed appetite for the pleasures of life was infectious. She quickly became my partner in prowling, the girl I blew off steam with when I wasn't busy trying to get through my freshman year at the University of Hawaii.

"I don't know if I want to get all sandy," I protested.

"Come *onnnnnn*," she pleaded.

I looked at Branden to see how he felt about this.

"You wanna go, right?" Cassie asked him.

He nodded.

"I *knew* I liked you. I'm Cassie, by the way," she said, flipping her hair and placing her hand behind her to signal her guy. "And this is Luiz."

Everyone made pleasantries as we walked out of Hot Tropics and into the fluorescent-lit parking lot—where the woman who had spoken to Branden stood at the driver's side of a white Camry. My body tensed at the sight of her. I suddenly felt wobbly in my stilettos. A slick layer of sweat above my lip betrayed the cool, confident front I needed for safe passage. Branden grabbed my hand as we passed her and I shifted my focus to him and smiled. I heard her car door shut and her engine start, and wondered what motivated her to speak to Branden. Was it a commitment to uncovering the truth? Did she believe that he deserved to know? Did she think about how he would react? And how was she certain that he did not himself know, or that I did not tell him? I still do not have answers.

I rode with Branden to the beach, where I walked with my

heels in my hands, crushing sand under my bare feet. Cassie and Luiz ran ahead, tipsily touching, leaving a trail of clothes for us to follow. They splashed into the water without care. The Pacific Ocean wasn't vast enough to cover their lust. I liked skinny-dipping because it was a group activity that alleviated the pressure to hook up. I found comfort in the black of night. I pushed my skirt down to my ankles and pulled my top over my head. I stood still in the raw, cool wind and my black lace thong. I had something to prove, so I slipped out of my underwear and waded into the water. I was nude but not naked, wrapped in an enigma that Branden would never figure out.

Forced disclosure always shook me, leaving me in a frightening space where my body served as proof of my realness. The need to prove myself valid was never-ending in its plea to affirm, connect, deny, and erase. I aspired daily to be like Toni Morrison's Sula, a woman who shuns the demands placed on her by her watchful community, a woman who lacks ego, a woman OK in her otherness. She feels no pressure to verify herself. Her only aim is to be consistent, not with the world or those around her, but with herself. On that beach, I was far from that place.

"You coming?" I teased, as I pulled my tiny brown braids into a knot at the top of my head.

Branden hurried out of his clothes and swam after me. When he caught up to me, I yielded, letting him touch my lips with his. Our bodies met under the warm, slow waves, and we stayed that way until daybreak, when I felt assured that I was leaving him without a doubt. *I once met a girl so fine women made up crazy-ass stories about her,* I imagined him saying to friends over drinks.

I don't know what happened to Branden. I never answered when he called. I didn't return his voice mails. It wasn't that I didn't like him. I just knew I shouldn't push my luck. But this was never about Branden, just one of many men who kept me company when I was young and seeking, who never went past the meet-cute or a few dates and nights in bed. I dangled myself like a charm, luring people close enough to push them away when things got deep. I vacillated between revealing and concealing myself. I preferred to be seen and admired yet unknown. Keeping just enough distance was the sweet spot, an intimacy disorder that allowed me to be present but far away. I let them in, my flesh being the means of exchange, but I never let them stay.

I trusted no one. I disappeared into myself. This left me alone with untruths that kept me company: *It's too dangerous for them to see you. Keep it close. Seal it tight. No one would want you if they truly knew you.*

GENERATIONS OF GIRLS HAVE been told that the only way they can survive is to remain silent, go unnoticed and blend in. If a girl was able to fit the narrow, nearly unattainable confines of what society demands women look like, it was expected that she keep quiet about her past and just pass. It is never far from my mind that some, not as fortunate as I, are often ridiculed, shamed, hurt, or attacked when they fail arbitrary tests that I seem to pass.

I've always taken issue with the term *passing*. It promotes a false impression that trans women are engaging in a process through which we are passing ourselves off as cisgender women—which we are not. We are not *passing* as women. We are not *trying* or *pretending* to be women. We *are* women, and cis people are not more valid, legitimate, or real than trans people.

Besides, to *pass* always felt like an insult when I was striving to *excel*.

Still, I benefit daily from the privilege of blending in and not being seen as trans. My womanhood is unchecked and unchallenged in most spaces that I enter—from the grocery store to the subway to the locker room. Because of my appearance, I am granted the choice of discretion, of actually choosing how open I am about my experiences, and that is a privilege many are not granted. They are faced daily with the burden of other people's ignorance and intolerance. We don't have to search for too long to watch footage of a girl being attacked on public transit or in the restroom, or read a story about the killing of yet another black or Latina woman. There are only so many vigils, so many murals, so many pleas for justice before we must succumb to the fact that our culture is intent on us not existing.

Yet so many still choose to survive, and that looks different for each of us.

I chose to wear the cloak of normality as part of my own survival. I wanted to be accepted as I saw myself, without rebuttals, without denial, without exile. I followed a prescription handed down to me from women I knew who had also benefitted from blending and passing. I took notes as a teenager watching these women slowly separate from their family and friends, leave their places of becoming, and start somewhere no one knew their name. They believed—no, they *knew*—the only way out was silence.

As these women fled, they took with them experiences and stories and knowledge that would not be passed on, wisdom that other girls would never bear witness to or benefit from. They went out and got *theirs*, because that's what they were taught was the only way to make a way. For years, I got *mine* by remaining silent and blending in. Now I've finally reached a place where silence is no longer an option for me. My survival depends on my ability to speak truth to power, not just for myself, but for *us*. I'm committed to getting *ours*. It requires me to relay how I struggled with living, dreaming, loving, fucking, being seen, and simply *being* in my body, in this world. *This* is a universal experience.

Since the release of my first book, *Redefining Realness*, many have written to me to express their amazement that I shed my anonymity and chose to be open. A common phrase I've read is *You didn't have to*. But long before I opened up publicly, I was just a girl making her way, searching for her voice, her purpose, and her place. Part of my process of self-discovery as a young woman depended on selective openness, which gave me the power to choose with whom I shared myself. This offered me space and time to figure out who I was without a facet of my identity leading the way for me. It delayed the process of having to navigate the limitations of others.

I have gotten the chance to choose to whom I tell my story, which has been a privilege that not many have been given. But our stories are ours. They belong to us, and we should be able to tell them—not at the convenience of others but when we are ready. Holding tightly to mine all those years complicated some friendships, romances, and relationships with classmates, coworkers, and roommates. My selective openness led to the end of some and the deepening of others.

Today I no longer deny or hide. I own my story. I enter spaces without leaving parts of myself behind. As much as I own that history, I also own the fact that for many years, I evaded and avoided my truth. Though I am aware that many might make better choices than I did and may now have access to better choices than I had, this book, *Surpassing Certainty*, describes the path I took as I figured out who I was and processed who I didn't yet know I'd become: the woman who thrives as a storyteller, an advocate, and a wife. This is my attempt to show up for that girl who is yearning to be let in, to be accepted, who believes that obscuring herself is her only possible gateway.

PART
ONE

ONE

I HAD PASSED CLUB NU routinely back when I was in high school. The bus that I would board after school to take me to my retail job at Pearlridge Mall used to drop me across the street from the strip club's door. It was an unremarkable sight, a dull blue shack with white bulbs that spelled its name on the facade. Located on the *mauka* side of Kamehameha Highway, an artery uniting Aiea to Pearl City and Waipahu all the way to the North Shore, Club Nu was a place most people overlooked on their way to the mall, Aloha Stadium, or Pearl Harbor naval base.

The shabby exterior was a front, masking the accessible glamour of its interior. Club Nu was a cozy haven for blue-collar guys. Within its plush-covered walls, paint-splashed construction workers, oil-spotted mechanics, and sea-salted sailors stationed a few miles away were treated as nothing less than kings. Regulars entered knowing how the booze and the generous, soft thighs of the club's harem of dancers would wash away their worries until last call. Or at least that was what the owner, a Korean woman the dancers affectionately and respectfully called Mama, wanted them to think.

Mama designed her establishment to be the laid-back alternative to the larger, wilder tourist traps in Waikiki, places where men would go primarily to show off their virility to one another, not simply to enjoy the attention of attractive women. There they paid girls to sit on their laps, then flung their bills onto bare asses to reinforce the cracks in their fragile masculinity. It was the kind of performance Mama believed most men didn't want, especially if what they really wanted was to unwind. Club Nu's clientele sought simplicity and intimacy, and Mama prided herself on her ability to deliver. Each customer had the opportunity to lure one woman from a curated assortment, who would look him in the eye, nod prettily, and giggle softly at his jokes throughout the evening. Mama's girls were encouraged to say yes, unless the customer couldn't control his liquor or his tab closed.

The sun hung low on the horizon when I first approached the front door of Club Nu in May 2002. A bald, bulky bouncer, adorned with a Maori panel tattoo that ran from his temple, over his right eye, ending at his jaw, greeted me from the stool on which he sat. He seemed intimidating, the way big local boys tended to do until their sweet high-pitched pidgin revealed their gentle-giant dispositions. His unblinking glance told me he had seen dozens of other girls just like me, in my cropped top and low-rise jeans, ready to be inspected by Mama. He didn't check the fake ID I held between my long acrylic tips, painted nude and embellished with small crystals as if I had dipped my fingers in cane sugar. He smiled, stood from his stool, and opened the door.

Club Nu's walls were draped in rich burgundy fabric that looked like sliced red velvet cake. Plush black booths lined the walls, and a stage beckoned from the front of the club. Each booth had a reflective metal table wedged between two leather love seats. This offered patrons both privacy and a view of the stage that on a busy night could entertain fifty people—ten at the bar, forty in the booths. The bar was perpendicular to the stage and the adjacent dressing room.

Onstage, a fortysomething Filipina swayed her body to the Eagles' "Hotel California"—the finale of her four-song set—as a dozen men enjoying happy hour looked on. She was the color of a butterscotch lollipop, with round breasts that could break a man's sweet tooth. Her long dark brown hair framed her slender silhouette, lit by neon—pink, green, blue, and yellow. She mouthed every lyric along with Don Henley, *Some dance to remember, some dance to forget.* Anyone half paying attention could tell that this song meant something, maybe everything, to her. I imagined her younger, long before her stage was set for dancing in the darkness, when she first heard this song.

Then, looking over at the bar, I locked eyes with Mama, the only person allowed to smoke in the club.

A slim cigarette rested between her red lips as her narrow eyes devoured me whole. Her unmoving straight hair was cut into a severe black bob and highlighted with red streaks, like embers refusing to let the foreboding darkness win. Her fair skin, taut over a moon-shaped face, was a beacon in the shadowy bar that shielded her fifty-plus years. Her eyes seemed to take in the parts of me that most reflected her younger self: a tight bare belly, lustful lips, and high-perched cheekbones, framed by thin, beyond-arched brows that displayed my ferocity and steeliness. Mama put out her cigarette in a glass ashtray and summoned me to the bar with a nod. As I got closer, I could see from her smirk that I was in.

"What you like drink?" Mama asked, as she poured a glass of soju.

"Oh, I don't drink," I said.

"Ah, because you're nineteen," Mama said, shaking her head, while taking back the glass she had slid toward me. "No good."

"No, I'm twenty-one," I said, sliding the ID I had bought across the bar.

She flicked her wrists in the air without glancing at my card.

"*I* give you two of *my* birthdays," she said, pulling out another shot glass. She filled it to the brim with the contents of the Korean-labeled bottle. "Happy, happy twenty-one, pretty girl."

Our glasses met and rang in celebration of my hiring. It seemed like the world's shortest interview. Upon reflection, I guess there wasn't much a dancer and a strip club owner really needed to discuss.

"You girls get *everything*, even if it break the law and give me gray hair," she said, winking. She lit another thin cigarette, matching the elegance of her lingering fingers. "Smooth brown skin, white teeth, long legs—what else could you ask for?"

Her question wasn't meant for me. She was having a conversation with herself. I gritted my teeth in pain as I sipped the stinging drink.

"No need," she shooed. "I know you don't like it. This is a woman's drink. You have to *live* to enjoy."

Mama took my glass, poured its contents into hers, and shot it.

"You start tomorrow."

I nodded, and she pinched my bicep before clacking away in Chanel kitten heels. The double-C logos sparkled under the bar's twinkling lights.

The dancer scooped up her bikini from the stage floor, and my girlfriend Cassie strutted out of the dressing room. She wore a tube top and a thong, both the color of sin, her jet-black hair collected in a high ponytail that snatched her eyes into tight slits. She focused them on me and grinned, giddy that I had gotten the job. She had persuaded Mama to interview me by telling her that I was a "good college girl" who'd show up on time, keep my mouth shut, and get the fake ID required to prove my age in case the liquor commission dropped in.

"Mama told me she could tell you'd be *no* trouble," Cassie said, placing a furry, scallop-edged rug on the stool nearest to me before sitting down.

"Thank you for making this happen," I said.

"Please! I'm just happy another *girl* will be here." She smiled. "So you start tomorrow, yeah?"

I nodded.

"Before you come back, get a rug like mine," she said, leaning over and giving me a better look at the three-foot-long and two-foot-wide piece of sheepskin that she lugged around like a prized feline. "Don't lie around this place bare. Always put something between you and the stage floor, the seats, and the booths. You never know what skank has been there before you."

I nodded as Cassie outlined the lay of the land. I would start on the slower early shift, six P.M. to midnight, until Mama said otherwise. The prime-time shift, nine P.M. to closing at two A.M., was reserved for dancers who'd earned her trust. The pay was twenty dollars an hour. We kept all our stage tips, which we used to tip the bartender, waitresses, and bouncer. Every dancer made fifty-percent commission on all drinks bought for her at the bar. A cocktail consumed by a client cost ten dollars (though the men generally drank pitchers of beer), but that same drink if bought for a dancer cost twenty dollars. Patrons were accustomed to paying this premium for a working woman's company. It was a system seen throughout Asia, known as *kyabakura* in Japan or simply hostess bars elsewhere, in which women offered their time, attractiveness, and conversation to men who compensated them by buying expensive drinks.

The brief silence between songs helped me calculate that even on the slowest nights, with zero tips and zero drinks sold, I could earn at minimum $120.

"Cassie!" Mama called, clacking her Chanels toward the bar. "Your turn."

Cassie rolled her eyes back to me as she teetered to the jukebox with the trusty rug in hand. I watched her as she inserted a five-dollar bill, which bought her four songs. She began her set with Sisqó's "Thong Song," her slim-hipped body stiff to the beat. She was a *hapa* doll, unclothed and unmoved, her high cheekbones like summits no man could ever climb. She looked no one in the eyes. The customers indulged in the parts of her body she wanted them to look at and open their wallets for. Two men, seated at opposite ends of the stage, held out fans of bills, hoping to entice her. She would not be beckoned. They would wait.

After my interview, I returned home to the two-bedroom apartment on Richard Lane that I shared with my mother and two younger brothers, Chad and Jeffrey. Jeffrey, who had just completed seventh grade, could most often be found on the couch playing his PlayStation or watching the Disney Channel (*Even Stevens* or *Lizzie McGuire*). Chad, on the other hand, was rarely home that summer, choosing to spend his final weeks in Hawaii with friends. He had accepted a football scholarship at Avila College in Missouri, becoming the second person (after me) in our family to attend college. He would leave home in July to begin summer practices.

My brother and I graduated from Farrington High a class apart—nearly three decades after my mother walked in her white cap and gown with my eldest sister, Cori-Ann, just an infant, in her arms. My mother, who is Native Hawaiian and Portuguese, grew up the eldest of six in public housing in Kalihi, a struggling neighborhood often dismissed as the "ghetto." I spent most of my childhood and adolescence in Kalihi, except for the handful of years when my parents were happy together in Long Beach, California. Those years were followed by their postdivorce period, when Chad and I lived with my father for most of my elementary school days in Oakland, California, and my father's native Dallas, Texas, where he still resides. In Hawaii, there was no surer way of letting locals know your socioeconomic status than by sharing your alma mater. Farrington, which was just a few blocks from our apartment, rivaled Waianae High as the toughest on Oahu. I was assured of my street cred.

I don't recall having a conversation with my mother about my new job, but she was never a helicopter parent, having raised us mostly on her own as latchkey kids whose comings and goings she rarely tracked. She took a laissez-faire approach to parenting that enabled me to do whatever I wanted throughout my youth—from wearing makeup and dresses as a tween without the raising of a brow, to ingesting hormones as a teen with limited discussion, to slyly engaging in the sex trade as a high school student, which provided me with the funds I needed to obtain medically necessary yet cost-prohibitive healthcare procedures, such as sex-reassignment surgery.

My mother, who worked as a contracts administrator downtown, rarely went out in the evenings. Chad didn't have a driver's license, so my mother's white Mazda was often available for me to use at night, as long as I filled the gas tank. I used it the day after my first visit to Club Nu to drive to a high-end auto-parts store near Restaurant Row. When I entered the store, I walked to a display of car mats and picked out a cream-colored rug that cost about one hundred dollars. The dealer, who usually sold these rugs in pairs to owners of SUVs, knew immediately that I was a dancer upon checkout.

It was a worthy investment in my new gig that I knew would fit neatly into my course schedule. I was about to enter my sophomore year. I hadn't yet declared a major but was intent on studying law because of my pedantic nature and my obsession with *Ally McBeal*. The quick money was also enticing. Though my college tuition and books were covered through scholarships, that wasn't the case for my mother's utilities, Jeffrey's PlayStation games, my weaves, my wardrobe, and my nights out. My earnings at Club Nu would help me pay for those necessities and have some spending money to spare.

I walked into the club at five thirty P.M., with my furry rug and a black tote packed with a collection of bikinis, some perfume, and baby wipes. The bar was empty, except for Mama holding court in a booth with three of her friends. A tall, thin white man with downcast eyes and an unconvincing side-comb stood near Mama. He held a broom in one hand and a dustpan in the other. I took him for the busboy or janitor, but I would learn that he was Mama's husband, though he was never introduced to me. The women all seemed to buy their thong sandals from the same bedazzled-obsessed designer as Mama; there was a Swarovski deficit somewhere.

"Meet my new girl," Mama said, placing her hand on my denim-clad hip. "Her name . . ."

"Skye." I jumped in, realizing that Mama was giving me an opportunity to share whatever name I wanted. I chose the one I had used on the streets.

"Your skin so soft," one woman said, touching my arm.

I smiled.

"You so pretty," another chimed in.

"That all your hair?" one asked.

I shook my head no, as my wavy auburn and blond hair brushed across my shoulders and back in generous, long layers. I loved nothing more than a fresh, just-pressed weave.

"Don't matter. You be pretty bald, too," she said, as the other women nodded in agreement.

"You get boyfriend?"

"No, she get boy*friends*!"

This vocal gawking went on for what felt like fifteen minutes. Mama didn't say anything. She just drank her soju and smoked her thin cigarette. This, again, wasn't a conversation. Like all the young women who worked at Nu, I was their vision board of youth remembered. I stood and smiled. That's what I was paid to do.

Mama looked at me as I shifted my weight from one leg to the other. "Go ahead," she said, pointing her cigarette toward the dressing room.

Cassie was the only dancer in the dressing room, seated on a bench in front of a well-lit vanity. She was in the middle of putting on a false lash strip. I was surprised to see her, because she was a prime-time Nu girl.

"Hey, girl," she said in a low tone, keeping her one open, already-lashed eye on her other in the mirror.

"Hey!" I smiled, excited to see her. I settled in next to her at the mirror as her lashes dried.

"So I got Mama to change me to the early shift," she said. "That way, we can work together. Plus, you'll get promoted to prime time in no time."

I knew this was not entirely true, because no girl would give up the profitable late shift without getting something out of it. I knew that Cassie was tired of being the *only one* in the space, even if she was the *only one* who knew it. Cassie was one of those trans women who could access spaces without being read as trans or, as we said colloquially, *clocked*. But no matter how *unclockable* a girl was, no matter how well she could blend in, she still carried that seed of fear about being found out. That seed had been planted in us both long ago, and we knew that the longer someone isolated herself, the wider those branches would grow.

Before Nu, we had been party-girl acquaintances. To be honest, I usually tried the best I could to avoid her. The handful of times we shared space over dinner, dancing, and drinks with mutual girl-friends—all young trans women—I could barely tolerate her. Her mouth was filled with labels. "Look at my new Chanel clutch!" "He bought me this Tiffany pendant!" "I'm dying for an Hermès scarf!" I wrote her off as a vapid label whore, too easily moved by luxury acquired by sugar daddies. We rarely engaged beyond a passing "Hey, girl." She kept me at bay, because my eye rolls were never subtle. Though I would come to know her as a girl who accessorized with dollar bills, she was quick to announce that her thongs and garters were all "from La Perla, thank you very much!"

Eventually, though, our similar journeys bonded us. We were both Hawaii girls who had grown up being called *mahu*, a Native Hawaiian identity that defined people who embodied the diversity of gender beyond the dictates of the Western binary system. *Mahu*, which loosely translates to "transgender," was most often used as a playground pejorative when I was a child. But its use in Kanaka Maoli (indigenous

Hawaiian) culture gave space and designation to people whose gender did not conform. *Mahu* were most often spiritual healers, caretakers, and hula dancers and instructors (or *Kumus* in Hawaiian) and are still visible in contemporary Hawaii, where multiculturalism has been the norm.

Growing up on Oahu (which translates to "the gathering place"), Cassie and I benefited from Polynesia's openness to various genders. I didn't spend my adolescence in isolation as most trans youth did. Instead, I was surrounded by a gaggle of trans girlfriends, including my best friend, Wendi, whom I transitioned alongside in middle and high school before she relocated to Las Vegas to be a makeup artist. Hawaii's community of trans women was vast, diverse, and deeply resourceful. The girls knew how to navigate ignorance, harassment, poverty, and various systemic hurdles to fulfill their needs. Cassie and I were just two of many on the island who had gone after our girl. I'd had my *change* in Thailand at age eighteen. Cassie had gotten hers in Montreal more than a year before me, when she was twenty-two. Now we communed at a strip club, sashaying between two poles, flaunting and covering ourselves.

My presence at the club provided Cassie with safety by proximity. And though it was unsaid, she had only brought me in because I passed the same subjective appearance tests that she had and because I was discreet.

"What's your favorite song?" Cassie asked now. "Something not too fast but not too slow."

"'Rock the Boat' by Aaliyah," I said. It was the song currently on repeat in my Sony Walkman. I was still mourning the singer's death.

"I'll fill the jukebox for us tonight," she said, lacing her strappy Lucite stilettos. "I'll take the first set, but after my first song, you go out, walk around, just play hostess. Then we'll switch on and off until more girls come at eight."

I watched Cassie strut out of the room in a blush lace bra and matching thong, her body willowy and straight, save for her full B-cup breasts. She was five-foot-eight and free in her bareness, like most girls I'd meet at Nu. I was still shy with my body then, especially in the company of other women. I felt that I didn't measure up, and this failure on my part made me feel illegitimate. However, in the company of men, with their coarse hands, broad shoulders, and protective biceps, I was generous in my nakedness.

I chose a brown Brazilian cut bikini with small turquoise stones dangling from its ties at my neck, back, and hips. Brown was my nude, so it gave off a bare appearance. I hadn't yet purchased those clear Lucite heels that seemed to complete every dancer's uniform. They looked tacky, and I couldn't escape my pop-culture association with them in the film *I'm Gonna Git You Sucka*, where the pimp, stuck in the heyday of the '70s, wears an extravagant pair of clear platforms with goldfish swimming in them. Instead, I sheathed my feet in strappy black sandals laced up to my calves.

I walked around the club to a few smiles and nods, but no one's gaze lingered. Every seat at the bar was filled, and half the leather booths were occupied with pairs of men, all heavy into happy-hour conversation. Cassie was shaking her uncovered torso with much effort to TLC's "No Scrubs," and the men couldn't care less. This was their end-of-day drinking hole, where the beer was cold and the girls were cute. I would learn that the men who came only for the girls waited until the sun moved off our island. That's why Cassie kept her thong on; she saved its removal for the tip-friendly customers.

After interrupting conversations between men at a few booths and forcing small talk (which I loathed), I was left with a deflated ego and no drink-buying fortune. Then Aaliyah's *hmmms* and *yeah yeahs* saved me from my awkward failings, calling me to the stage like a sultry siren. I stepped onto the neon-lit platform and slithered my way to the shining silver pole, each stiletto pouncing to the beat. My sheepskin rug dangled loosely off one of my nails, sweeping the floor. My free hand clutched the pole, my only dance partner, with the peering eyes of Mama's gal pals my only attentive audience.

TWO

FULLY UNDRESSED, CASSIE WAS SEATED onstage on her rug engaged in floor work. She was opening herself up for Shamari, one of the most bankable babes in the club, and one of Shamari's many regulars. The man stared at Cassie as if he were in a trance, sipping his beer and pulling a bill from one of the two four-inch-high bundles of cash stacked before him. Shamari, a former Marine from Texas who had been honorably discharged for reasons still unknown because she never spoke to any of us backstage, was the color of molten gold, with dark brown hair. She was about five-foot-five and had the kind of curves that would make Ja Rule name-drop her in his next song—ample derriere, thick thighs, and breasts that sloped to perfection.

Floor work was arguably the laziest task a dancer had to perform. It basically required you to sit, squat, or get on all fours in clear view of men sitting at the tip rail as if they were about to give a gynecological exam. You spread your legs or bent over to show the details of your lovely lady labia. Club Nu was not your local titty bar where the big reveal was a dancer removing her bikini to unveil her generous and shapely breasts. It was an all-nude, bottoms-off spot, where men lined the edge of the stage to meet a woman's lips. Floor work was most often the finale of a dancer's set. You never revealed yourself prematurely; it was about the art of the tease. You summoned customers from their comfortable seats to the tip rail with one article of clothing at a time and the promise that you would be bare soon.

Shamari and her regular were close enough to smell Cassie when she rose from her behind, turned around, and squatted on all fours. As Shamari sipped her Hennessey from a frosted glass, I could see her eyes, as green as a kitten's, looking at Cassie with the marked boredom of a woman uninterested in any pussy but her own. She glanced between Cassie's legs because not to do so would have been rude. Shamari's client was transfixed as Cassie bent over in performative desire. I hated it when girls, even dancers, sat at the tip rail. It brought out my deepest insecurities that another woman would see me and immediately know something was not quite right, like a Saint Laurent bag from an online dealer in China.

BEFORE CLUB NU, I had never been to a strip club. The only dancers I knew before Cassie were girls I'd met when I hustled on Merchant Street as a teenager. They worked at big flashy clubs in Waikiki and would come to our stroll on slow nights to earn a few late-night dollars. We viewed these women as legends. They were *unclockable*, blending effortlessly into the narrow confines of externally defined womanhood: they were shorter than five-foot-eight, with average-size feet and hands, slim waists, curvy bottoms, and delicate facial features. No one questioned their womanhood. They went undetected. Because of this rare access, they were nondisclosing in most spaces; they lived, for a lack of a better term, *stealth*. They kept their origin stories to themselves. They navigated the world with the confidence that *no one knew.*

There are undocumented thousands who have transitioned and

lived some form of *stealth*, some going as far as severing any ties with anyone who may have known them before they transitioned. *Stealth* requires trans people to blend in at all costs, including breaking away from their places of becoming, leaving behind those who knew them *when*, isolating themselves, and strategically hiding or recreating their histories. Many hid and continue to hide because they were taught that being openly trans was impossible—even dangerous.

Cassie and I were *stealth* at Club Nu. Mama wasn't running one of those late-night revues that Honolulu used to be known for, which boasted on marquees, "Where Boys Will Be Girls." No, it was a club that served booze and nude (assumed-to-be cis) women to straight men.

Dancing in the club gave me greater confidence in my body, particularly enabling me to appreciate the aesthetics of my vagina. I had long feared that mine did not look "normal," as if there were a standard look for all vaginas, and in my mind, I thought normal equated to the picturesque pink blossoms that were neatly folded and delicately layered. These were the polished pussies of *Playboy*—smooth, without layers or complication. They looked untouched by life, vaginas birthed from male fantasies. Comparing my trans girl vagina with these airbrushed images only heightened my insecurity. I wasted so much of my youth measuring myself against things outside myself. It was at Club Nu that I was exposed to vaginas from all walks of life. Some were juicy, flappy, slim, fat, thick, slack, compact, and variations in between. No two were identical, yet all belonged to women.

The only fear that continued to follow me when I was dancing was the thought that either my mother's brothers or someone unfriendly who had known me *when* would walk through Nu's doors. My uncles and my maternal grandfather, who, like most of my family, were supportive of my transition, were the only adult males present during my adolescence, and I would have felt as if my own father had shown up. It would have been a mutual shaming. I would have been embarrassed for them to actually see me onstage in nothing but a thong, performing in this dancer role—a job they did not know

I had—just as it would have been embarrassing for me to witness them in their horniness. Luckily, the men in my family rarely left the comfort of their front porches, satiated with Heineken-filled coolers and marijuana-filled medicine bottles. To them, strip clubs were rip-offs.

Then there were guys with whom I had gone to high school. A few times, I vaguely recognized former classmates who came by, avoiding eye contact with the trans girl they'd had geometry or sociology with. I sensed their curiosity when I was onstage or seated in a booth with my hand in a customer's lap. I would try to read their thoughts. *I wonder if he knows.* My only choice was to be a pro, to feign that I was in control and that this was my space and that they were on my turf. Everything had to appear normal for the facade to work, to make them feel at ease with the information about me that they had in their grasp. If I showed any sign of insecurity, I knew they could and would transform the elephant trunk in the room into a trumpet.

Otherwise, I felt little shame about dancing. I was raised in a culture where strippers or women who appropriated the stripper aesthetic were not hidden but actually displayed. Glorified in hip-hop music videos on MTV (from Tupac's "How Do U Want It" to Nelly's "Tip Drill"), these women danced, strutted, and twerked. They were positioned crotch-, ass-, and breasts-first for the viewing pleasure of men, overwhelmingly used as set dressing to endorse a musician's manhood and desirability.

I stood in awe of these women who seemed empowered by their bodies and sexuality—even if it was all pretend or for pay. Years after I left the club, I started noticing even more empowering displays of strippers, most often helmed by women in the mainstream. Women like Rihanna (the "Pour It Up" music video) and former dancers Blac Chyna, Cardi B, and Amber Rose ("That was the best time of my life!" Rose told *Cosmopolitan* magazine. "I was young, beautiful, I was onstage, I wasn't really ashamed of my body. I made lifelong friends.").

Women like Beyoncé, who sang an ode to dancers with "6 Inch" on her iconic album *Lemonade* (*She works for the money . . . And she worth every dollar*).

But no matter how many celebratory images of strippers I sought, there was still commentary that aimed to shame dancers. Chris Rock's voice rings loudly in my ears. The comedian has been unrelenting when it comes to degrading dancers. His bits have gone on to become stripper sound-bite legend. In his 2004 comedy special *Never Scared*, Rock says one surefire signal of failed fatherhood is the sight of your daughter on a pole:

> *Sometimes I am walking with my daughter. I'm talking to my daughter. I look at her. I'm pushing her in the stroller. And sometimes I pick her up and I just stare at her and I realize my only job in life is to keep her off the pole. Keep my baby off the pole! I mean, they don't grade fathers, but if your daughter is a stripper you fucked up.*

Not all women working in strip clubs were pushed there because of some parental failure, and only a patriarchal society would claim a woman's profession—respectable or not—reflects on the man who did or didn't raise her. Our culture is obsessed with raising perfect little girls who are virginal and virtuous and respectable in their womanhood, girls who do not dance on poles, trade sex for money, or THOT around town seeking pleasure. Choice and circumstance led the women I worked with to the club. We were all driven by a desire to take charge of ourselves and to take care of our families. These women took responsibility for their lives, their bodies, and their babies in a culture that offers limited resources or opportunities to women living in low-income communities of color.

Backstage was where I'd overhear calls home in which mothers, young and old, would coo into the phone or scream at an ex for not showing up, for missing another child-support payment, for always disappointing. Backstage was where I listened to the world of women grappling with love and loss and romantic narratives and hopes for the future. Backstage was where we laughed at the desperation of patrons, swapped shifts when someone's childcare fell through, or offered to give someone a ride home. My feminism is rooted in the conversations I had backstage where these working women spoke it plain and persevered.

Women displaying themselves publicly can be seen in art galleries, on the silver screen, and on cable television, but it is the woman under the glare of neon lights who is singled out and told that she should be ashamed of herself. What's so corrupt about baring your own body to support yourself? Racialized sexism only further exacerbates this double standard, which gives white women like Dita Von Teese greater freedom to profit from their nakedness and achieve mainstream success but limits the opportunities for women dancing in clubs in the hoods of America. A white woman splashing around naked in a human-size martini glass to entertain rich people is worthy of applause and magazine spreads, but a black or Latina woman trying to make a living doing the exact same thing with a pole is dismissed as a ho unworthy of protection, care, and respect.

Rock's comedy is not solely to blame, though; he merely amplifies our culture's misjudgments. In *Never Scared*, Rock continues to belittle women who view stripping as a transitional job during college:

> *What I got a problem with is the stripper myth. The stripper myth is: "I'm stripping to pay my tuition." No, you're not. There's no strippers in college. There's no clear heels in biology. Shit, man, I didn't know they had a college that took one-dollar bills. And if they got so many strippers in college, how come I never got a smart lap dance? I never got a girl that sat on my lap and said, "If I was you, I would diversify my portfolio."*

Most strippers I knew were not paying for tuition; they were paying to survive in a world that shamed them for monetizing their sexuality, something our culture demands to be available and free.

Though I had access to affordable education and didn't *need* to be in the club, it was a convenient part-time job that enabled me to make money quickly while carrying a full course load. For me, stripping seemed like a promotion from my sex-trading tenure. Dancing nude was a more regulated and safe space in the sex industry. Plus, I was nineteen, learning to enjoy my own form, riding high on the male attention I didn't attract openly in high school. I relished being swooned over with dollar bills. It was a no-brainer to take my clothes off in exchange for money.

IT TAKES MORE THAN a handful of body oil, a glob of glitter, a dozen pairs of gooey lash strips, and a few pairs of Lucite heels to make anyone an exotic dancer, a showgirl, an adult entertainer, a nude girl. Becoming a stripper was much more than looking the part. There was no stripper uniform. Sure, the sheepskin rug that followed me as I walked the floor in my clear stilettos definitely aided my transformation. But becoming a stripper also had to do with the way I slid my hand across the shoulders of men to ensure that I got a few rounds of drinks, the way I took shots of watered-down tequila, the way I swayed my hips to pull a man's wallet toward my body.

Mama did not want us hopping from customer to customer. Her dancers were selective and loyal. She believed that a woman who provided intimacy, who put in the time, could turn any newbie, any faithful husband, into a Club Nu regular. She designed a space where we were not competitive and the clientele was not rushed. We were expected to sit and flirt and bat lashes and convince. She believed women had the gifts of gab and gams and that those two things made a man pay up. It took time. That was why she paid us by the hour. She knew that if we were not worrying about quotas, we would sit and talk and rack up bar tabs. Sex was not for sale; intimacy was.

I played a character in the club, a girl whose sexual availability was perpetually on the horizon, just out of reach. I cut a hopeful, teasing image that lured men with the possibility of penetration. It was this dangling possibility that helped a dancer build a roster of regulars. It was all about getting a man who was infatuated with you to believe that if he came back and bought you a ton of drinks, maybe you'd get drunk enough to let a lap dance or a champagne-room romp go a bit further. But it went way deeper than mere sexuality.

Your duty was to be amiable, available, and flirtatious. You were to make a customer feel comfortable, interesting, and attractive. Much of the work involved listening and talking, crafting open roads in conversation that would stimulate him, inflate his ego, make him feel centered and listened to. It was the emotional labor of a therapist, really. While drinking alcohol—even though my drinks were most often diluted with water or juice—you had to hold on to story lines, names, characters, and developments, especially for regulars who returned to you.

I lit cigarettes, ensured that their drinks were always poured to the brim, that their tables were wiped clean, that there was a laugh at the end of every joke, a nod after each statement. You were selling a girlfriend experience—the fun, warmhearted, yet undeniably attractive girlfriend they could whack off to when they returned home to their empty, or often occupied, bed. They knew it was an exchange, and they were content to pay a premium for cocktails because that came with this service. You sat and talked and rubbed thighs, all while getting the waitresses to bring round after round of drinks that left a man with a tab of three hundred to five hundred dollars, of which you took home half. Sleeping with a customer was forbidden, because all it would do was limit your earning potential and hurt the reputation of the club. It was more profitable to have a steady spender, even if he was not exclusively spending on you. Having him return meant there was money in the club, and more money in the club helped every girl's bottom line. Besides, sleeping with you was the fantasy you were selling, and if you gave him the reality, the fantasy would be shattered, and he'd move on to another dancer in another club. Though you were not having sex with him, your attractiveness and sexual availability were a commodity.

My aesthetic in the club was 1970s black goddess glam, a cross between blaxploitation icon Pam Grier and disco queen Donna Summer. I was brown, backlit, and bodacious. It took me a few months to realize that I was not dressing for myself or for other girls the way I did outside the club. The neutral colors that I gravitated toward offstage would not help my rich brown skin stand out under the dim lights. Browns and creams made me blend into the darkness. I needed to stand out. Color from a Hawaiian floral shop would become my uniform. I collected a duffel bag's worth of bikinis in white, fuchsia, turquoise, and even lime green and highlighter yellow. The brighter the color, the easier it was to lure a paying customer, like a fisherman using fluorescent bait in muddy waters. My goal was to glow as the darkest girl in the club. Back then, my ass could easily fit into a Brazilian cut bikini, and my firm breasts sat perkily in barely-there triangles, more like slits that basically covered my nipples.

I'd sit at the bar between sets, sipping orange juice in short-shorts and a bikini top, looking like a music-video extra, waiting for my song to call me to the stage. When those sultry beats summoned me, I would rush to the dressing room, baby-wipe inside the front of my bikini, spray myself with Clinique's Happy perfume, and grab my sheepskin rug. Onstage, I'd lay my rug down, grab the pole, sway my hips, and walk around the pole like a show pony. I'd scan the audience, targeting the man who was still looking after the first minute, the one who didn't return to his sudsy drink or his chatty friend. I would cradle his stare and let him know that he was all that mattered. He'd be convinced that the girl on the stage was dancing only for him.

Two more songs would play, and he would likely be too shy to leave the privacy of his booth. I wouldn't mind if he stayed seated, because I was intent on seducing him to let me join him after my set. He would buy me four to ten drinks, earning me forty to one hundred dollars. Over those two hours, I would dance for him again, and this time, he'd sit at the stage, tipping me five-dollar bills during my four-song set. We'd return to the booth, and the time between my drink purchases would widen, signaling the moment to move on.

When I thanked him for his time and made him promise that he'd come back to visit me, he would usually leave with his expectations for a quick night of fucking flattened.

A different man, fueled by booze and a sense of entitlement, would argue. "Come on, babe," he'd say. "I bought you all those drinks."

He would feel he deserved more attention, more time, having bought my uninterrupted attention for the night. Laughing at his jokes was not enough. Letting him feel my upper thigh was not enough. Letting his rough pinkie occasionally rub against my bikini line was not enough. He demanded more of me, more of my body. That's when I'd upsell with a private lap dance, which cost twenty-five dollars a song. The average client bought three consecutive private dances, just enough to get him off. A lap dance was basically a handjob in which you used your entire body, and because of this commonly held truth, Mama didn't take a cut of our lap dances.

My physical boundaries were simple: No penetration. Period. Regulars were allowed light petting and fondling privileges. If I was hovering over one during a lap dance, he could rest his hands on my hips or push his face against my breasts.

Most regulars were respectful. They kept their hands and tongues to themselves. They had their own rules of engagement. Regulars tended to wear chinos, shorts, or sweatpants—never jeans, because denim was too thick and rough. They wanted to feel your touch when you rubbed your body against theirs. The thinner the fabric, the closer they were to you. They entered the club with the initial intent to scout and survey the place. They'd grab a drink at the bar (the club didn't charge a cover, but it had a three-drink minimum) and watch the dancers. They were looking for an attractive woman, of course, but more often, they wanted someone who smiled onstage or laughed with a fellow patron. They wanted a good-time girl who seemed to be enjoying herself, who had a softness to her appearance.

They avoided blatant hustlers at all costs, the women who walked around the club as if they were predators looking for meat. Regular customers recognized that all the girls were there to work, but they wanted it to be an even exchange, one in which they would not leave feeling completely used by a dancer who pulled her garter out every few seconds, soliciting tips or drinks.

Regulars usually took about thirty minutes to scout, and then, once they had their eyes on a dancer, they would take one of two actions to see if she was available. They would either take a seat at the stage and tip her in larger bills—mostly fives, tens, or twenties to relay their spending power—or they'd settle into a booth or the bar, order a drink from Mama, and let her know they wanted to buy a drink for the woman onstage. Mama would then hustle over to you backstage and let you know you had a client waiting.

Regulars were most often on their best behavior, because they ultimately wanted a stress-free experience. They also knew that strippers at Club Nu were a sorority, and Mama's dancers looked out for one another and the good of the club and spoke freely about all patrons—the good, the bad, and the pervy. A guy with a less than favorable review from a dancer could be spotted in any club. He would be the one sitting alone at the bar with a beer, wondering why no one had approached him. It was because word had spread that he was too grabby, too stingy, or too creepy.

You could also spot the veteran dancer. It was more than merely her age. She was easiest to peg when it was slow in the club and there was a lull between clients and her set. She was the one sitting alone at the corner of the bar, her legs crossed, sipping a drink. You could tell she was a pro by the look in her eyes. She was alive, but she was not engaged. It was almost as if she were numb. I had that look, which was a mix of protection, performance, and disengagement. In her 2010 stand-up special, *Money Shot*, Whitney Cummings talks about women who have seen too much yet still have to feign interest because their livelihood depends on it:

> *I had a guy say to me once, "I want you to strip for me." You want me to be emotionally unavailable and take your money? I've been doing that since we freaking met. All I need is some self-tanner and a shitty sun tattoo and I'm ready to rock this right now. Let's go: Dead eyes!*

Over that summer and into the fall, as I began my second year of college, the neon lights started to illuminate my perpetual boredom. It might have been exciting at the beginning, but this became my routine from Wednesday to Saturday during the prime-time shift at Nu. Dance. Seduce. Repeat. There were no girls doing backflips on the pole, no girls getting rained on by dollar bills, no girls starring in music videos. Just the sound of Mama's clacking heels against the black tile floor as she shepherded girls from the dressing room to the stage, broke large bills for tips, unlocked expensive bottles of champagne from behind the bar, and distributed twenties to girls clocking out.

THREE

I SPENT MY FINAL MONTHS as a teenager in expectation, waiting for something to happen. If you had passed me then, I would have been looking beyond you. My head held an inch higher than its usual resting place, my eyes lowered just a bit, my chin tilted just so. You would have believed I had grown up anchored by happiness and stability, care and wholeness. A sense of entitlement hung over me, and for some reason, I expected things I'd never seen, never felt, never experienced.

I waited, confident that something, someone, would come. I was unapproachable as I sat in waiting. I gave off an impenetrable air that challenged young men and made them stifle their desire with prideful proclamations: *She ain't all that. Stuck-up bitch. She saving it for a white boy.* I was young and insecure, safer behind a protective front.

I refused to admit that I was lonely.

One November night, six months into my stint at Club Nu, I sat on a barstool lined with my sheepskin rug, watching Mama sip her soju.

"Slow tonight for you, yeah?" she asked.

"Yeah, but it's fine. I did good last week."

"My good girl," she said, raising her glass to my orange juice. *Clink!* "You never give Mama worries. That's why *you* my favorite." It didn't take much to be deemed Mama's favorite. You just had to do as she said.

It was past midnight on a Saturday, and I hadn't even made half my goal of ten drinks. I returned the juice I was nursing to the bar and asked for a splash of vodka. If anything, I could leave with a buzz. Then, I saw him enter the club.

I looked past the wrinkles in his white T-shirt and the basicness of his cargo shorts to his rosy cheeks and his steady blue eyes, as clear as a cloudless sky. He resembled Matt Damon, with broad shoulders, blond hair, and smile lines that creased the edges of his eyes. I was struck by the swagger in his stride, which I would learn disguised the knee injuries that had drawn a curtain over his former football fantasies. His limp remained, though—a nod to black cool.

This white boy's got swagger, I thought to myself from the bar, eager now for my set to begin. I had never been in a rush to take the stage before. I wanted to dance, just for him, to show my goodies, treats I was sure I'd be sharing with him that night. *Was he that thing I had been waiting for?*

I have never wanted someone as intently as I wanted Troy that first night. He did nothing to deserve my unyielding desire. I'd crossed boundaries I had set in the club to satisfy regulars, teasing empty promises of pussy if they got me another drink or letting their noses slip into my panties during private dances. But no one in Club Nu knew my real name—not even Mama—and no one could say he had taken me to his bed.

Troy would know my name. I'd never seen him, so I framed him as a newbie and danced as if I was his first. I wanted to show him what he'd be lying next to later. And he knew I would bow in his bed. The quiet, smiling, boyish-eyed thing made girls like me feel secure and free in their sexuality. We could control a man like him, we thought. He made us feel sheltered in our eagerness to unveil ourselves to him. But behind that smile and those twinkling eyes was a knowing glare; all he ever had to do was show up to draw us in.

He sat at the edge of the stage, staring up at me. His neck was exposed, and I felt powerful knowing I could grab it, kiss it, bite it. He was as vulnerable and open as he was strong. I swayed my hips before spinning and squatting in front of his face. I was bold in the command of my body, twisting and bending and undressing as he looked at me.

"Why are you here?" I asked, sweeping my long hair over my right shoulder.

"Bored, I guess," he said, in an unbothered way that only increased my desire.

After my first song, I told him to leave the stage because he was bad for business, like a boyfriend glaring over a client's shoulder during a lap dance. At Club Nu, I didn't belong to anyone; I belonged to everyone. Availability was currency, and I flaunted that myth during my next two songs before making Troy buy me a drink.

"Mama! I want tequila and pineapple, please," I said, pressing my belly against the cold metal of the bar.

The corners of Mama's eyes creased. "Tequila?" she asked before pouring. She knew most of my drinks were watered-down.

I nodded.

"Twenty dollars, sir," Mama told Troy.

He handed her the money and looked at me quizzically, unsure if he was being hustled. When he saw me sipping the drink leisurely, he felt reassured. For me, the drink was a cover, justifying my sitting and talking with him. This was our beginning lit in neon lights, surrounded by women with stretch marks and concealed C-section scars. We were marked by life, decisions, and mistakes.

Troy told me while sipping a Corona that he had joined the Navy nearly four years before. He was twenty when he enlisted, with hopes of becoming a SEAL, but his bad knees prevented entry into the elite program. Instead, he settled for an administrative position as a yeoman. He found that his attention to detail worked well in this job, and he could listen to music at his desk as he worked. Pearl Harbor was his first duty station, and he thrived as the right hand to one of the highest-ranking naval officers in the Pacific fleet. He felt pride in being valued but didn't feel fulfilled in a desk job, filing and shuffling papers, when he had been physical his entire life.

When I finished my tequila, he asked if I wanted another.

I shook my head. "Why don't you get out of here," I whispered in his ear, "and I'll call you when I'm done?"

He wrote his number on a cocktail napkin as I stood up from the booth. I walked to his side of the table and pushed my thigh to meet his face. He pulled my lace garter and slid the napkin onto my flesh.

It was difficult getting through the remaining two hours of my shift. I was distracted by a flurry of dissonant thoughts. I was hungry for his presence yet irked by my hopefulness. *Who the hell meets anyone in a strip club?* I asked myself. Our romance seemed doomed from the start. Still, I knew I would do something I had never done before: hook up with a customer. I was breaking a cardinal Club Nu rule. It was an unspoken restriction Mama put on her dancers. But there was something different about Troy that didn't allow me to see him as a customer. This made it easier for me to rationalize crossing the line.

I drove to Troy's apartment, just five minutes up the road from Nu, confident in my decision to be with him. I swapped the fuchsia bikini I'd been wearing when I met him for a black maxi skirt, a white tank, and flat gold sandals. As I pulled up to his building—a high-rise with lanais, a doorman, and a pool—he was standing in the visitors' parking lot and directed me to a parking spot. He opened my door and kissed me deeply before I could step out of my mother's car. He tasted like mouthwash masking beer.

Upstairs, I straddled Troy on a couch in his living room, which overlooked Pearl Harbor in the distance. It was dark and quiet. My lust for his body made me overlook the emptiness of his apartment, particularly his bedroom, where he laid me on a mattress with a white bedsheet and a single pillow. The mattress made a hissing sound as we lay on it, feeling each other, into each other, through the night.

In the morning, I picked up my clothes in his barren room, hoping to sneak out before he woke. But the zipper of my skirt betrayed me.

"Come back here," he said, patting the empty space that had held my body all night. I couldn't resist his sleepy eyes and pleasure-filled smile.

"I have to get home," I said. "My mom needs the car."

"What if I followed you and brought you back?"

No one had ever uttered sweeter words to me.

In my rearview mirror, I sneaked glimpses of Troy in his black Jeep as I drove home to Kalihi, where the roosters were still in conversation with the rising sun. My mother walked into the kitchen to turn on the coffee maker as I gathered a change of clothes and some toiletries from the bathroom we all shared. Jeffrey, ever the late riser, was still asleep in Mom's room. The three of us had grown into our own rhythm in Chad's absence, carpooling to school and work on weekdays and watching one-dollar matinees at Restaurant Row on Saturdays. My mother also looked on without judgment as I slipped out of the house with her car keys for shifts at Club Nu and tiptoed through the house in the middle of the night. The aroma of vanilla macadamia nut coffee filled the house as my mother watched me walk out of the apartment yet again without a word.

Troy and I returned to his bed in Aiea and just looked at each other. Our faces were new, just-discovered territories we were eager to explore. I don't remember us talking much. He was a quiet man, agreeable and desiring. His bare bedroom became our lovers' den for the next three days.

I called into work, and Mama knew it wasn't because I was sick or overwhelmed with my course load. She knew it was because of the *haole* boy.

"No fall in love," Mama told me over the phone. "You're young. Beautiful no last. Be smart, girl. Make money. Save. Love can wait."

She knew dancing was a young woman's game. It was as fleeting as physical beauty often is. She consistently told us to be smart, to plan, to concentrate on making and saving our money. But that day, I heard her say, *Save love*. It was what I wanted to hear, no matter how out of character it was for a woman who was not sentimental. I took it as encouragement to stay there with Troy as long as he'd have me.

Besides, love could not wait. We were not promised forever. This, too, could be another fleeting experience if I did not care for it and invest all of myself in it. Each day, we made love when we woke, after we ate, and before we slept. Our only duty was to explore our bodies, bodies I felt were made to connect. We sat in the dew of each other with no desire to move from what we had created. We cleaned each other only to get drenched all over again. I had never wanted someone's skin against mine as much as I wanted his.

I had given parts of myself to men for passing pleasure before this. I had lent my body to men, grasping onto myself out of protection. With Troy, I surrendered and finally learned what it meant to make love with someone. I was falling.

We subsisted that weekend on sex, stares, pizzas, and plate lunches. Though I was energized by the possibilities, I had a life to return to, work to be done, classes to study for. I told Troy I needed to leave, and he looked at me as if he were about to cry.

"Stay," he pleaded, pulling my rising body down into his strong arms.

I obliged, because no one had made me feel so wanted and necessary. It was the first time I felt I could be enough for someone.

"I think I'm falling for you," I whispered, as we spooned. It was easier to say these words with my back turned to him. It was as if I were sending a wish out into the world, eyes closed, heart open.

"Me, too," he returned.

We had only known each other for three days. I felt possibility and promise. I knew he was the one. There was no other explanation for the way I fit in his arms, the way my flesh tingled with his touch, the way I felt sheltered in his unyielding embrace. I had never felt this way before. It was overwhelming, and my stomach began to ache. I shuddered.

"Is everything OK?" he asked.

I nodded, trying to shake the familiar discomfort away. But you can't escape your truth. It follows you. No matter how far you travel, how good you feel with it at a distance, it lingers and sticks to you. I felt an urge to blurt out what he did not know about the woman who had been laid up with him over the weekend. But I didn't want this—whatever it was, whatever it could be—to end. So I clutched my stomach and forced myself to shift the conversation.

"So you've been in Hawaii for three years, and you still don't have bedroom furniture?" I teased.

I could count the contents of his room on one hand: a TV and PlayStation on a table, an open suitcase with clothes, and a mattress on the floor. It seemed like a dorm room or a barracks—bare, sterile, temporary. I thought how lucky he was to meet me, a woman who could help him make a home. When I turned to look at him, he wasn't smiling with me. His face fell.

"Yeah. About that," he started.

I sat up and covered my bare chest with his white sheet. I fought my brows, which wanted to furrow in deep concern. I didn't know what he was withholding from me, but I told myself just to listen.

"I wanted to tell you when we met, but if I did, you wouldn't be here right now," he said. "I didn't want to blow this."

"It's OK," I lied. "Just tell me."

"All right. I'm moving. I got orders six weeks ago, and my stuff was packed up for Australia a few days before we met."

I wasn't surprised by his revelation. I was used to people coming and going on Oahu. It was a migratory population of tourists, wealthy people with time-shares, and enlisted military personnel like Troy. He had been in Hawaii for three years. He had planned to be here another year but had chosen to leave his post early in order to follow his commanding officer. He had joined the military to see the world. He always knew there was more out there than his small town in Maryland.

I felt as if someone had kicked me in the stomach. The air was sucked right out of me. It took me a few minutes to process that this deep infatuation, the only thing close to love I had ever felt, was temporary. I could not frame Troy as a fling or a brief affair. He felt like something so much deeper. I felt cheated.

"I'm sorry I didn't tell you earlier," he said. "When I went into the club, I never thought you would be there. I was just going in because I was bored.

"And there you were, talking to me, paying attention to me. You weren't hustling me for tips or drinks. You were interested in me, and I just thought there was no way you'd be with me.

"All I knew was that I wanted to talk to you as long as you'd talk to me. That was it. I didn't have any expectations. I didn't come there to pick up a girl.

"But I knew, Janet," he said. "I never wanted something as bad as I wanted you. You are the most beautiful thing I have ever seen."

There was no response but to kiss him. I could not punish him for not having considered me before he even knew I existed. I told myself to make the best of the time I had with him. Weren't a few weeks of bliss better than none?

My disappointment turned into relief when I realized I didn't have to tell him that I was trans. If it was just a few weeks, what did it matter? My past was none of his business if he was leaving me anyway.

He is not staying, I told myself. I steeled myself to be the tough, detached girl again. *You are alone.*

Still, I was buoyed by the prospect of us spending Troy's remaining few weeks on Oahu together. The hopefulness I felt about our courtship energized me, enabling me to go from his bed to the stage to the lecture halls at UH. There is an energy to being young and in love. Your body is able to take on so much. It is forgiving. I can't recall getting much sleep when I spent those nights in Aiea with Troy. We spent most of our time together cuddled in his bed, watching rented DVDs, eating takeout, and making love.

It felt like a betrayal when I had to prepare for the stage on Thursday, Friday, and Saturday nights. Using his bathroom vanity, I applied my foundation, bronzer, blush, powder, and false lashes to transform into Skye, the girl he'd first met. He'd drop me at the back entrance with a kiss and a smile.

"Don't fall in love with anyone now," he'd say, winking as Mama opened the back door to the club.

I shook my head to shake him off me. It was the only way I would leave with money in my garter belt. I had to mask the girl inside, the one biting her French manicure tips off, anxious to get home to her guy.

Knowing that Troy was waiting to pick me up was comforting, but it made it difficult to entertain, to flaunt my body, to feign sexual availability. I no longer felt at ease with my place in the flesh trade. I was never one to meditate much on what was proper or improper, but taking my clothes off for other men now felt duplicitous. This body was and would always be solely mine, but now I was sharing it with someone else, and he was not in the room. For the first time, I felt I *belonged* to someone.

One Saturday night, I left early through the back entrance and saw Troy, his eyes nearly disguised by a cap he wore low. He was leaning out of his window, waving for me to hurry. I skipped over to him and kissed his pillowy lips. Our smiles refused to fall. I couldn't believe that I could be this happy and make someone else happy. I closed my eyes and wished to myself that time would slow down. I wanted him here for as long as possible.

"I got news," he said, as I closed the car door.

"What is it?" I asked.

"I'm not going anywhere." He turned toward me. "I didn't want to tell you until I was absolutely sure."

"Stop playing with me, Troy! There's *no* way."

"I *made* a way," he said with swagger.

Technically, he still had a year left in Hawaii, and his assignment in Australia was voluntary. No one could force him to go. Because he dealt with paperwork all day, he had gone back to his own and discovered that his knees were on record as prohibitive to sea duty, which would require him to travel up and down ship stairwells when deployed. He had made an appointment with his physician and gotten orders for rehabilitation, which enabled him to pull out of his deployment Down Under and complete his tour on Oahu.

"Will you have me?"

I screamed "Yes!" as if I were accepting a marriage proposal.

FOUR

I USED TO WATCH MY CLASSMATES in envy as they began pairing up in middle school. Passing notes, holding hands, locking lips—simple pleasures I wished I could enjoy. I believed a girl like myself, though, would never find someone to do those things with her. *Who would stand beside you—in public—and call you theirs?*

I tried my best to outrun that lovesick girl, the one who spent Saturday mornings curled up on my mother's couch watching basic-cable cuts of my favorite romances. *My Best Friend's Wedding, Pretty Woman, Waiting to Exhale, Sixteen Candles, When Harry Met Sally, Coming to America, Breakfast at Tiffany's, Woman of the Year.* My harsh reality faded into fantasies of a well-dressed, city-filled adulthood where true love loomed. These films made me feel good. They were reliable, like that best friend who never fails to grab your hair just as you're about to regurgitate the night's bar tab. She shows up no matter how pre-vomitus she is herself.

These Hollywood romances shaped me with promising thoughts: the overlooked girl is the prize; the hard-hearted can be softened;

happy endings start with a revelatory kiss; and ultimately love conquers all. The discovery that *no one* trips and falls into the arms of the love of their life was a truth I resisted. I knew it was Hollywood make-believe, yet I held on to the hope that someone would stand strongly and proudly beside me.

When Troy showed up, I thought he was a temporary reprieve. I was convinced that because he was leaving, I wouldn't have to share myself with him. It was easy for me to dismiss disclosing when he was moving to another continent. I would not go deep as we shacked up together during Troy's final days on Oahu.

My rule about disclosing was simple: Tell when it's serious. I had never been in a serious relationship. I had never been called someone's girlfriend. Without the possibility of longevity, I was not compelled to share my story. My only experiences of disclosing happened early on in my transition. When I was sixteen, a year into my medical transition, I began to notice that people no longer stared at my body in confusion. They no longer questioned my gender, because I began to present more clearly as an American girl. Unbeknownst to me, I was suddenly successful at passing. I was blending in. This was my teenage dream: to be seen and accepted as just another girl. With my gender nonconformity seemingly fading away, I began to attract the attention of men.

Though I grew more and more comfortable in my body and with my looks, I hadn't grown comfortable navigating spaces of desire. I had no experience—boys in class never flirted with me, none of my male peers hit on me. So I didn't know what to do when attractive 18-to-24-year-old cisgender heterosexual men began to stop me on the street and tell me I was pretty. I didn't know the correct protocol—or if any existed—when they flattered me without prompting and pleaded for my phone number. Back then, I would disclose almost immediately—usually over the phone—before accepting an invitation to dinner or a movie. I was deathly afraid that a guy would find out I was trans and hurt me. I didn't want to join the twenty-plus trans women killed annually in the United States—the second most dangerous country behind Brazil to be trans, according to the Trans Murder Monitoring (TMM) project. My fear was only heightened by my small-town surroundings and the fact that I had yet to have bottom surgery. Disclosing up front seemed like the safest possible option.

As I grew more confident in my body, gained more experience dating, and underwent bottom surgery, I began to see disclosure not so much as an obligation but as a gift. My story was mine, and I felt a person had to earn the privilege of hearing it. Random suitors and passing dalliances were no longer *deserving* of me or my story. But Troy proved himself deserving. His presence was no longer fleeting. He grew to become much more than a farewell affair. He was staying *for me*.

I had never had a boyfriend before, but that's what Troy was. We didn't have a conversation about not seeing or sleeping with other people. It was unspoken that we were there for each other, that no one else would enter. With that assurance, I began the process of figuring out Troy's tolerance level for difference, for anyone who did not conform. I wanted to see how open he was and how accepting he could be. There were limited portraits of trans people on television (and it was rare to find affirmative stories), so I could not see his reaction to their presence there. Having that would have been anxiety-producing for me anyway. So I had to use queerness as a stand-in.

I began with reruns of *Will & Grace*, a sitcom that centered on the friendship between a gay man and a straight woman. Troy watched and laughed at the antics of Jack and Karen, who really were the true stars of the show. He seemed to genuinely enjoy *Will & Grace* along with me, watching all parts of the show, from slapstick scenes to romantic story lines, even ones between Will and his partner, Vince. Kissing scenes between men were seen without an utterance of vile commentary. If he had expressed homophobia, I knew there was no way he'd be open to the possibility of being with a trans woman, and if his homophobia showed itself in a verbal tirade or physical revulsion, I would know it was time for me to pack my overnight and return home to my family. But gay people living and loving did not seem to threaten or offend him. He had a blasé, "do you" attitude. He seemed to recognize that they deserved to live their lives freely without his judgments.

It was an imperfect system, but most systems are when they're created in isolation. There was no outreach group or center I could rely on to help me navigate dating and disclosure as a college student. In high school, I attended a monthly support group for trans students called Chrysalis, which was a rare safe space where we shared our experiences as young trans women. There was no equivalent to Chrysalis at the University of Hawaii. The only resources available to trans women in Hawaii dealt with healthcare, HIV/AIDS, and substance abuse. There were no resources that supported trans women in intimate partnerships with cis straight men. There still aren't, so we continue to do this work in isolation.

Troy was broad, sturdy, and strong, but he moved around the world without notice. He had a quiet confidence, a gentleness that made me feel secure and safe. He was not boastful or arrogant. He didn't center himself or take up space. He was assured in his own presence. All of this together gave me confidence to begin teasing out information about myself in the hope that he would see me and still love me. I wanted to put him in touch with deeper parts of me.

I was not a beach girl. I grew up with a mother who was born and raised on an island yet did not know how to swim. She could not stand the way sand stuck to everything, so we rarely took the twenty-minute drive to the beaches that people from the mainland spent thousands to visit. Troy was drawn to the water. We spent our first few Saturdays together on the sand at Waimea Bay, where we began revealing and sharing parts of ourselves.

It started with Spam. For Troy, Spam was white-trash food, canned meat that was grocery-store filler. His doting Italian mother, who ensured that her two sons went to school with a hot breakfast, wouldn't dare serve it at her dining table. In Hawaii, Spam had its own displays in our stores. It was a daily presence on plates of locals who ate more than six million cans annually. I was raised on Spam glazed with brown sugar and *shoyu* cooked in a skillet with eggs and rice. I ate Spam fried rice as well as my absolute favorite snack, Spam *musubi*, which is a slice of grilled Spam placed on top of a block of rice held together with a sheet of dried seaweed.

Local food made me feel at home. It was a signifier of my Hawaiian culture, and sharing some of my favorite dishes was a means of sharing myself with Troy. I was committed to having him taste my Hawaii, and it started with Spam *musubi* on the beach.

"Trust me, you're gonna love it!" I said, as I removed the plastic wrap and handed it to him.

"OK, I'm trusting you," he said, as he grabbed it.

I watched him clench his teeth around a quarter of the *musubi*. He chewed the meat, rice, and nori apprehensively before taking a second, enthusiastic bite.

"*Humph*, not bad," he said, with a wide, satisfied smile decorated with black freckles of seaweed on his white teeth.

Spam *musubi* soon became part of our beach trips, packed into the cooler we carried with us in the Jeep. I shared other local cuisine, our favorites being *lau lau*, *kalua* pork, and *malasadas*. He even came to look forward to rice and mac salad with his mixed plates, with *loco moco* being his default brunch order—a hamburger patty, fried egg, and brown gravy over a few scoops of sticky rice.

For Troy, music was a gateway to knowing him. He exposed me to genres I would have never considered enjoyable. I was raised almost exclusively on R&B, from Anita Baker and Luther Vandross to Jodeci and Whitney Houston—powerhouse black voices. I did not venture far from that, hip-hop, and Top 40. My knowledge of music was limited to whatever my father had on his cassette player in the early '90s or the countdown on MTV's *Total Request Live*, which dominated my

teen years in the early '00s. Troy's tastes were diverse. He had dreamed
of being a radio DJ, someone who'd break the barrier of single-genre
radio stations. Loving the Roots and Goody Mob as much as Dave
Matthews and Audioslave, he grew frustrated by the color line in the
music industry. His passion was contagious. He made me want to
know more, and I would listen intently and appreciate the lyricism
of the artists he played during our long drives to Waimea Bay. Jack
Johnson, a local boy from the North Shore, became an early favorite,
enabling the quiet man I was falling in love with to express how he
felt for me.

"When I was younger," Troy said during one of our trips home
from Haleiwa—we were eating shave ice from Matsumoto—"I never
used to take my shirt off when I swam. I was a chubby kid. I didn't
want to embarrass myself, you know."

I quieted my slurping as he continued to open up to me about the
insecurities he felt in his own body.

"And I still kinda feel weird, even though I'm a grown-ass man,"
he said, laughing, "but having you next to me, it feels all right. It feels
good."

I grabbed his hand in gratitude for sharing this revelation. I had
never suspected that he felt insecure about his physique, which was my
ideal. He was built like a football defensive player, with shoulders that
expanded over me. I felt privileged not only to bear witness but also to
have been part of his process of reconciliation with his own body.

Inspired by his openness, I decided to free myself from a long-
held insecurity that had cost me thousands of dollars and countless
hours. The following Monday, when Troy was at work, I sat at the foot
of his full-length mirror and untangled my hair from the hundreds of
braids that protected and lengthened my own hair. I pulled a fishtail
comb through each thread and unwound a strand of curls at a time. It
was a meditative process that took three hours, leaving me with a bag
full of kinky hair weave and a three-inch-high curly fro.

I ran my fingers through my curls and massaged my scalp. It was far more satisfying than the weave pat I had grown accustomed to over the years. It felt equally good to stand in front of the bathroom mirror and see my hair as it was—without a weave, without a flat iron, without manipulation. I usually only sat with my own natural hair for the few hours it took to wash it, condition it, and refashion it. This time, I was in no rush to control or contain it. Instead, I cared for my hair. I washed and deep-conditioned my curls. I rubbed coconut oil onto my head. I slowly detangled my curls and styled them with a thin elastic headband. Years of extensions, braids, and heat had loosened their pattern. They refused to settle into perfect spirals or loop the way they were supposed to. They twirled at the root and limped lazily at the ends.

Growing up watching black women swinging long locks had convinced me that I needed to control my curls by melting and molding them into shape. It didn't help that I had grown up in Hawaii around Asian and Polynesian standards of beauty that did not make space for my dark looks and kinky locks. Filipino girls I grew up with in Kalihi had black stick-straight hair. Samoan and Hawaiian girls flaunted brushed-out waves that cascaded down their backs. As a teen, I coveted what I didn't have and yearned just to fit. I forced my hair to get in formation.

My teen idol Beyoncé taught me that my hair could take as many shapes as I wanted. She made me feel emboldened by the adaptability of black-girl hair. I spent my teen years emulating her ever-changing looks—micro braids, cornrows, long highlighted weaves, chic high ponytails. She taught me that ours was freedom hair—we had the freedom to do with it what we wanted.

As I threw the bag of hair down the trash chute, I panicked, struck by a wave of insecurity and regret. *Am I still pretty? Can I pull this off? Will he still like me?* By the time I met Troy, I had shifted from a long auburn weave with honey highlights that framed my face in cascading layers to brown micro braids that allowed me to give the hot comb a break. I loved the way long, wavy hair hit the middle of my back, the way it moved in the wind, the way it lay on my cheekbones and shoulders. But there was no mane to shield me. I was anxious as I sat on Troy's bed waiting for him to return home from work. I busied myself with episodes of *Sex and the City*, which I had begun to binge-watch with rented DVDs. Troy got home a little after four P.M. and stood in the doorway looking at me.

"There you are," he said, as he beamed his wide smile. "Can I touch it?"

I nodded sheepishly, visibly insecure without the protection of those long locks. I turned to the side, posing against my shoulder in a way that obscured his view of my face. I was afraid to open up straight to him. He had never seen me like this. No one but my hairstylist had. I felt exposed. He took my face in his hands, looking me steady in the eyes, and kissed me. I felt he finally saw me, not the sexy girl onstage.

That was the start of my natural-hair journey. Hair is political and personal. The way we wear our hair is a statement we make about ourselves. I'm not one of those people who have deep opinions about how other women style their hair, because it's *their* hair. What I do know is there were a lack of images of women with hair that grew up above their heads, occupying space, daring to stick out in a world that was forcing all of us toward sameness. It took me years to grow comfortable with my curly fro—and myself.

That night over sushi takeout, Troy looked at me and said, "I love you, Janet." His statement was muffled by the *ahi poke* that filled his mouth.

I knew that love was more than a statement. It was an action that required accountability. I was thoughtful about my response and knew that in saying I loved him, I had to get out of myself.

"I love you, too." I smiled. He kissed me and returned to his chopsticks.

When we finished dinner and began to clean, I felt it was finally time for the truth. He deserved to know me.

"Troy, I can't have kids," I said over the sink. I was rinsing plates for him to load in the dishwasher, and I made the statement without much thought. "I know that's a big deal for some people."

"Not for me," he said, wiping his wet hands with a rag.

I felt reassured but knew that we were not at a point in our relationship to consider children. It was the one thing I could not physically deliver that many women can. But I was just beginning to reveal myself.

"When I was younger, I struggled with something that I didn't have words for," I said. "I spent my childhood confused, trying to figure out what exactly was wrong with me, even though there was *nothing* wrong with me—medically speaking. Then I met a doctor who helped me. He told me I was not crazy. He gave me words to identify and describe my feelings.

"He helped me find solutions, and things became more and more clear, and I began to feel more at ease with myself. At eighteen, I had surgery that made me feel *truly* comfortable with my body.

"Then I met you," I said, trying to see and read Troy's face, which was obscured by my tears. "You're the first person I've ever loved, and I just want to be honest with you, Troy. It's not something that I share with people. It's hard for me to talk about it, but you deserve to know this before . . . I don't want us to go any further with you not knowing."

My vague telling of my transsexual journey forced him to fill in the blanks without putting labels to it. I realize now that I refused to give my experience a name. I rejected labeling myself in his presence, because I did not want him to see me as anything other than the woman he had fallen in love with. I wasn't exacting with my language, because saying that I was a transsexual would have qualified my womanhood.

I thought that deliberately stating that I was a trans woman—a woman who hadn't always been seen as a girl or a woman and therefore had to fight for her right to reveal herself—would have only lumped me in with the tragic trannies who consistently sashayed across my screen as modern-day freak shows: the silent or sassy and hypervisible streetwalker; the tortured serial killer skinning cisgender women into a "woman's suit"; the awkward forty-plus "baby trans" giving up the benefits of white male privilege; the unclaimed maimed body. These skewed images only heightened the shame I felt about being trans. I aimed to separate myself from those pervasive portraits, absent of any affirmation or celebration.

I wanted to escape the stigma, and for Troy to see me as an exception.

He was attentive as I revealed myself on my own terms. He was generous enough to withhold any questions he may have had. He didn't press me for clarity. I hadn't had enough distance to reconcile with my past. I hadn't traveled far enough to own who I was, and he had the emotional intelligence to recognize that. He knew—and I don't know how he did—that this was all I had and could say. He did not demand more, and that was a gift.

"It doesn't change how I feel, Janet," he said, grabbing me by my waist and pulling me to him. "When I said I loved you, I meant it."

I had told the broad strokes of my story to someone I cared about, and he chose to embrace me. I was naive enough to believe that we could go on unchanged, that what I had to say didn't limit his visions for *us*. At the time, I felt loved and seen. It was a pivotal first for me. Troy gave a young, insecure woman struggling to face herself a valuable present by remaining steadfast, by being a person of his word, by showing me that I was worthy. He taught me that it was safe to trust and that what I had to say was not grounds for dismissal or disposal, which is all too common for many trans women seeking partnership. Men like Troy were exposed to the same images of trans women that I was exposed to through popular culture. I wasn't sure if he had internalized the demeaning messages of those images or if he just passively consumed them. *Did he pity trans women? Laugh at us? Was he repulsed?* There is no universal reaction.

All I knew was that he remained by my side. For this, I will always love Troy.

He was only three years older than I was, just settling into his own as a young man in the world when we crossed paths. He didn't yet know what he wanted in life, but he knew he wanted me. I was a vision of a future that felt right. I felt the same thing about him. He prided himself on being a good person, a person with integrity. He said he loved me, and he knew that meant something, especially when it allowed me to feel safe enough to let him in.

Could I go back on my word? he surely thought to himself.

Troy was born without a father, who left when his mother was pregnant with him. Troy felt unwanted and abandoned by the man who had been tasked with raising and shaping him. At twenty, his mother, Linda, was left alone to raise two young boys. Troy did not want to be like his father, a man who was not steadfast in his commitments, who would desert people who depended on him. Then his stepfather, Alan, came along when he was a toddler and stepped up to fill a void. He did so by showing up—always. He made Troy's mother smile, and he cared about Troy and his brother. Alan gave Troy a blueprint of a man of integrity that he could follow.

I believe Troy thought of these two men when I opened up to him. He faced a crossroad: *I could be my father or my dad.* He decided to be a man who showed up, one who opened up his heart and home to me. I moved in shortly after that conversation, and we settled into our own routine as a couple. I dropped him off at work at eight A.M. and sat in traffic during my morning commute to Manoa for classes. I felt cheated from a college experience at the University of Hawaii, because it was largely a commuter campus for locals like myself. I didn't attend football games or volleyball matches. I wasn't politically active in the campus demonstrations that were spreading after our peers were being deployed to Iraq and Afghanistan post-9/11. Instead, I did my work as if it were a chore and excelled in my core courses.

In the spring of 2003, I decided to give up on my dreams of living Ally McBeal's life. I could barely stay awake in a required philosophy course and accepted that a prelaw course load and I were not compatible. I felt deflated by this reality and decided to treat myself by taking what I vainly saw as a fun, easy elective. I chose an intro course in the Apparel Design and Merchandising program. It was taught by a buyer at Neiman Marcus who moonlighted as an adjunct professor. I respected the real-world experience she brought to class, paired with her unbothered air and chic styling. She didn't take herself or the fashion industry too seriously. She made fashion accessible and dispelled the myth that her job as a buyer was all about being able to shop for pretty clothes all day. Being a buyer seemed like the perfect combination of aesthetics, practicality, and influence. Spending the semester with her convinced me that working in fashion was a viable option for me, one that fit neatly into the life I saw for myself as a young professional in New York City.

After declaring myself a fashion merchandising major, I met Lela, a fellow merchandising student with a major case of the prettiest resting bitch face. Her presence imposed on you. She was much taller and broader than most local Japanese girls, with long chestnut hair, tan skin, and almond-shaped eyes that never lost their sharp, pointed edge. We connected after being paired for a class project, and she disarmed me with a toothy grin that easily took over her entire face. If you weren't lucky enough to see her smile, you'd misjudge her as pretty, popular, and privileged, the kind of girl you envied because she seemed to have everything. Though she had gone to private school and grew up in Hawaii Kai, an upper-middle-class suburb on the east side of Oahu, Lela supported herself through undergrad by working at Christian Dior. She ranked as one of the district's top salespeople. We bonded over our dreams of working in fashion in New York, and she quickly became my first college friend—the only one privy to the details of my relationship with Troy and my evening job at Club Nu.

The only time my domestic routine with Troy—morning and afternoon carpools, dinner dates and deliveries, movies rentals and lovemaking—was interrupted was when I stripped on Thursdays, Fridays, and Saturdays. As I went natural, I spent a few hundred dollars on a long auburn wig with blond highlights. It resembled the layered weave I used to wear. Troy, a white man who hadn't grown up with black women who invested money in their hair, didn't understand why I spent so much on a human-hair wig. He thought my natural hair was cute, but I was going for sexpot in the club. A close-cropped curly fro didn't align with my vision of a bombshell. I could not swing my curls onstage. They did not sway seductively across my naked body. They did not flip and tickle the faces of tipping clients. The wig became an integral part of my dancer uniform, drawing a distinct line between Janet and Skye.

Working in the club, going to school, and building a home life with Troy began to feel onerous. When I sought a sympathetic ear, my girlfriend Cassie was not having it. She worked in the club, slept half the day alone, shopped for the other half, and returned to the club at night.

"Janet, you have a man, *and* you go to college," she said, rolling her eyes. "Stop complaining. You're living the dream."

But I felt as if I were doing double shifts. The emotional labor of listening to men, cuddling men, and giving them the intimate experience of companionship was wearing on me. Before Troy, it was easier dealing with the demanding hungry hands of clients. Now their collective touch felt like a violation. It felt as if they were always grabbing at me. I could no longer feign excitement when a longtime regular bought a three-hundred-dollar bottle of champagne for me. The money was no longer as attractive as it had been, because I was giving them *me*—my time, my attention, my focus.

I came home one night and told Troy that I no longer wanted to dance.

"Did something happen?" he asked.

"No," I said. "I just *can't*. It's draining."

I didn't expect Troy to understand my frustrations about the club. He thought it was a plush gig, where I brought home upward of a thousand dollars a week for hanging out in a bikini. He didn't get that it was work. Troy responded with silence. It would become a common response when he wanted to avoid a difficult conversation. He had a low tolerance for conflict and preferred to remain neutral or not engage at all. I wanted him to tell me it was OK and that he had us financially. Instead, we left it there, and I slowly reduced my schedule, from three nights a week to two nights to one. Mama was reluctant to let me go—especially since I didn't bring drama and was one of only two black girls in the club—but she knew I was taking my bow. She knew the gig wasn't a forever job, especially for girls with degrees and boyfriends on their horizon. Troy didn't comment on the fact that I was showing up for fewer shifts, and he remained silent when I just stopped showing up by spring finals. After a year at Club Nu, I hung up my Lucite heels, sheepskin rug, and wig.

That March, after three months together, Troy and I celebrated my twentieth birthday at the Spaghetti Factory at Ward Center, where he officially met my family. My mother and thirteen-year-old brother, Jeffrey, had seen Troy before but had never truly engaged with him beyond a polite smile and wave in the parking lot when I lived at home. That night, he was being introduced to the entire *ohana*. In addition to Mom and Jeff, we were joined by Grandma Pearl, Aunty Lisa, and Aunty Shane and their three and six children, respectively. Our party rounded out at sixteen. Troy, who was one of two boys, with no nieces and nephews, was taken aback by the commotion we collectively caused. People spoke over one another, grabbed children just inches from injury, took bites from one another's plates, gossiped about those not in attendance. He wore a nervous smile the entire dinner, one that is frozen in my first photo with him and my family. In it, he's standing behind me with one hand around my hip, his face flushed with beer and nerves.

Troy eventually grew comfortable with my family's large gatherings. He defended the honor of the Redskins with my uncles, die-hard 49ers fans, over Heinekens. He communed with Jeffrey during video games and boogie-boarding. He treated my mother and brother to movies and dinners on the weekends, laughing and talking easily over noodles at McCully Chop Suey.

For my birthday, Grandma Pearl gave me a card signed by her and Papa, with a crisp fifty-dollar bill. Aunty Lisa spoiled me with my first designer bag, a monogrammed Coach tote. Mom handed me two cards, one from her and another signed by both of my brothers, which meant a lot to me in Chad's absence. Troy bought me a DVD box set of the first four seasons of *Sex and the City*. He attached a birthday card in which he wrote the lyrics to the Dave Matthews Band's "I'll Back You Up": *Do what you will, I will back you up.*

A few weeks later, Troy received orders for his next duty station.

FIVE

THE FIRST MOVIE I SAW that resembled my own love story was *Soldier's Girl*, a film based on the relationship between Barry Winchell, a twenty-one-year-old private first class in the Army, and Calpernia Addams, a Nashville-based transgender showgirl. It was affirming to watch a romance unfold between an openly trans woman and a cis straight guy, but, like most depictions of trans life, it ended in tragedy, with Winchell being beaten to death by a fellow soldier as he slept in his barracks.

It confirmed something I had already known all too well: we are inconvenient women to love. I watched the film alone twice in our apartment before watching it a third time with Troy. I didn't tell him that I had already seen it. I acted as if my channel flipping were serendipitous. I watched him as he watched the Showtime movie.

"Damn, that's fucked up," he said at the end.

"I know," I said. "It's scary out there for most girls."

He remained silent, sitting on the carpet at the base of the bed.

"It's part of the reason I've always been so grateful. I'm lucky to have you."

"Don't get all sentimental," he said.

"I'm not. I couldn't help but think of us watching that."

"Really?" He seemed to be taken aback.

"Yeah," I said. "She's a girl like me, you know."

"Nah. You two are *completely* different. I would *never* date someone like that."

The transgender character on-screen—played by Lee Pace, a cis male actor, with great depth and tenderness—did not turn Troy on. She was not his type—too tall, too flashy, too Southern. Troy instinctively separated me from the movie version of Addams, an attractive woman who reminded me of a star from the golden age of Hollywood, because he did not see her as real. He was protective of our relationship. I don't believe he allowed himself to recognize that my journey was closer to Addams's than it would be to any of the women he had previously dated. This was something about me—the woman he loved—that he didn't comprehend and was resistant to understanding. He hadn't known me *when*. He only knew me *now*, and, unlike the cis actor on-screen, the woman he loved was not playing dress up. He was also protective of his identity and manhood, which dictated that "real men" date "real women." To venture out-side those confines—to desire a woman who had not always pre-sented and been seen as one—would shatter the rules he had been taught to abide. He was adamant about distancing me, us, from what he saw on-screen.

"Yeah, I know we are different," I agreed. "But think about how hard it must be for her to have found someone only to have him taken away."

"Oh, yeah," he said. "Shit happens."

My hope to use the film to have a deeper conversation about us—about me—was squashed. In the months since I had told Troy, he had never brought up the fact that I was trans. There were times when we bumped into girls I had grown up and transitioned with, and he never batted a lash. Maybe he was giving me what I thought I so wanted then: the guise of normality. As we grew closer and our time in Hawaii came to an end, I discovered I wanted him to ask me questions, to hear more about all I had been through. I held a unique set of experiences that differed from those of the women Troy had dated before, and this didn't make me any less of a woman. I was learning to become more assured in that, but I couldn't articulate it then. All I knew was that I was ready for him to express his curiosity, which I felt he *must* have. You don't spend that much time with someone and not wonder about where they've been and how those experiences shaped them.

It would take Troy months before he asked me explicitly about my past. It started with an innocent question about my father, whom he hadn't met or spoken to. My answer led me down a winding path where I retraced my childhood with my dad. I relayed the conflict between us over the fact that I failed to perform boyhood the way my father craved. I was sensitive about using the term *boy* in front of Troy, but he didn't flinch. This made me all the more comfortable to share my experiences in more exacting terms and details. I told him that I had known at a young age that I was a girl. I told him how I had gone head- and heart-first into my transition beginning in the seventh grade. I told him how I hustled to make the money I needed in high school to pay for vital healthcare that was not yet covered. I told him about boarding a flight alone at eighteen for Bangkok.

TROY WAS SET TO move to San Diego to work aboard the USS *John C. Stennis*, a nuclear-powered aircraft carrier that housed more than six thousand sailors. It was basically a floating city with a twenty-four-hour airport. He would finally see the world, one of his initial draws to joining the Navy over the other military branches. He respectfully concealed his excitement as I began to mourn our parting. I couldn't believe that this, that we, could be nearing an end.

I realize now that Troy was preparing his good-byes. He loved me, but we were not meant to last beyond Hawaii. I couldn't see it then, because I was so in love with him and so in love with love. I could not imagine letting go. What I took from those Dave Matthews lyrics, a song that still makes me think of Troy fondly, was that he would always be with me. What he meant to tell me was that he would always support me, no matter the distance, that he'd never deny what we shared and how he felt about me.

But I was not ready to say good-bye, and I fought for us by trying to find a solution. I had always been someone who was ambitious to the point of stupidity. When my mind was set on achieving or obtaining something, I'd most often take action before thoroughly thinking about the repercussions. It was my strength *and* my weakness. Troy's orders propelled me to sign up for a student-exchange program for my junior year. I did not want to be left behind in a place where I'd be reminded of him everywhere I went. There were only two schools, in Texas and Rhode Island, that participated in the program and offered class credits that would be transferable at UH. I chose the University of Rhode Island, because it was closer to New York City, on which I had developed a fixation in large part resulting from my love of curly-haired, navel-gazing Keri Russell in *Felicity* and my *Sex and the City* obsession.

When I told Troy that I would be moving to the mainland in the fall, it relieved him from the guilt he felt about leaving me behind. But I could tell that he saw this parting as the end, that Rhode Island was my adventure, San Diego his. He was not thinking of *us*. His focus had become singular, and I feared that I would be remembered as a girl with whom he had spent his last days in Hawaii, not a great love. Troy's orders helped him prioritize himself. He shifted his focus to his future, his career, traveling the world, and I shifted mine to maintaining our connection. I was committed to *us*.

I left Hawaii a week before Troy and arrived in Kingston, Rhode Island, in late August, when the locals were soaking up their final days of summer on the beaches of nearby Narragansett. Unlike the University of Hawaii, the University of Rhode Island had a thriving campus culture in a picturesque setting. Most students lived on campus or in nearby rentals. I was placed in condos reserved for exchange students. My roommate was an Irishwoman who had attended school in London. She had coordinated her academic year in the States with a few other U.K. friends, and they arrived as a tight clique who regularly hosted wine and cheese parties. She seemed to subsist on those pupu platters alone. Though I was cool with her, we were not close. We both seemed to agree that it wasn't necessary to become best friends just because we had been forced into close quarters. It was a pleasant, no-drama, good-morning, good-night roommate relationship.

The first person I connected with at URI was Sam, a girl in one of my marketing courses. She had a cello-shaped figure and a gorgeous heart-shaped face. She was one of the prettiest women I have ever seen, but she did not recognize that, because she didn't fit into the teeny mold forced on many white women. She was from a small town in Pennsylvania, where she had grown up the eldest of four, making her the responsible one, the designated driver. She rented a room in a sorority house, since on-campus housing was limited. Unlike the majority of the women there, she had no plans to pledge, yet her small room became a gathering place that attracted young women from all over. It was common for Sam to spend a big chunk of her time listening, nodding, and handing over tissues or her candy jar. She was maternal that way.

My friendship with Sam introduced me to the wider campus culture at URI. AOL Instant Messenger (AIM) became our base of communications in a pre-texting, pre-Facebook, pre-Twitter world. We gathered in group chats, gossiped, planned what we were wearing, relayed grievances or giddiness, and coordinated our daily schedules. Nothing was more important to me than my AIM status, which I changed at least three times a day—sometimes using quotes, other times stating my location and shouting out friends I was having a ball with. It was a vein connecting us in intricate ways.

Though I was a domestic exchange student, New England was a new world to me. It felt foreign yet familiar. Growing up in Oakland, Dallas, and Honolulu, I had always been surrounded by people of color. My friends were black and brown, Polynesian and Asian. My family was black and Native Hawaiian, lived in the hood, grappled with poverty in public housing, attended underresourced schools, navigated drug culture, and made do with minimum wages. In the places I came from, particularly in Hawaii, whiteness was not celebrated or centered. I grew up with a mother who often seethed when confronted with unchecked white privilege: *Ugh! White people think they know everything.* They were met with suspicion from my mother and my maternal and paternal grandmothers.

So it was discombobulating to suddenly be surrounded by whiteness in a moneyed college town in New England. But the white women I spent my time with at URI were not completely foreign to me. I had been watching women who looked and spoke like them on television since I was a kid. I adored women who looked like them, from Rory and Lorelei Gilmore and Carrie Bradshaw to Felicity. I was under the illusion that because my girlfriends accepted me, the overwhelming whiteness of the campus would not accentuate my otherness.

No one spoke about race on campus—not openly and deliberately. This was pre–Black Lives Matter, a time when we were not connected in conversations outside of our real-life space. Social media were not yet broadcasting the thoughts, essays, and activism of social justice. Despite this silence around race on campus, the lines were drawn between white students and black and brown students. I saw it every day in the dining hall, where black, Cape Verdean, and Latino students carved out their own spaces shielded from the majority white students. These racial lines were drawn in social life, as well, where Greek life and sports dominated.

Football parties were common in the fall and were often mixed gatherings, unlike frat parties, where the hosts were mostly white men who left their doors open for attractive white girls and their friends. Jared, a white wide receiver who was in our marketing class, threw the first party I attended with Sam. Jared sat in the same row of the lecture hall as Sam and I. He was handsome, with dark brown hair, thick brows, and a crooked smile that was cute and mischievous. I was attracted to him, so I often let eye contact between us linger a few seconds too long. He made my belly flutter, but flirting from a distance was my limit. I was committed to Troy, with whom I talked daily.

Sam and I attended the party with a few girls from the sorority house. I wore a white tank top, low-cut jeans, and brown sandals with my matching denim Baby Phat bag. (Please do not judge. It was 2003.) I was feeling myself. My eyes were lined, my cheeks bronzed, my cleavage popping, and my curls spiraled to perfection. But I was eclipsed by the three highlighted blondes I walked in with. I stood no chance. We scoped the scene in the three-bedroom house, which was crowded with about a hundred students. Most were gathered on the back deck around the beer pong table and the kitchen where booze lined the counters.

I filled my red plastic cup with cranberry juice and cheap vodka, while Sam, who was our designated driver, sipped on a can of Coke. The crowd was mixed, with black and white football players and the girls who were hooking up with them. *Hooked up* was a euphemism I had never heard until I engaged in mainland college social culture. It signaled that you acted on your attraction. It went beyond holding hands and chatting on AIM. It was a slut-shaming-proof expression that relayed that something sexual transpired. The girls I had grown up with had been exacting about what went down: *We fucked. I blew him. He munched me down.* I learned to resist the urge to ask, "'Hooked up'? But what did you *do*?"

Women outnumbered the men at the party, which created a competitive dynamic among girls gathered in their cliquey clusters on the perimeter of the house, all waiting for a guy to approach and engage. I was only one of maybe ten women of color at the party. I stood out from the mass of blondes and was still overlooked for them. Beauty is a social experience, subjective and interactive. When I was growing up, words like *beautiful*, *pretty*, or *attractive* were not regularly tossed my way as descriptors. When *beautiful* was used to describe me, it was often qualified through filters of gender and race. If they knew I was trans, they would often say, *Oh, my God! You look like a real girl*. If they didn't know I was trans, it would often be racialized: *You are pretty for a black girl. Oh, my God! You remind me of* [insert name of black celebrity].

For a black girl in Hawaii, my standard of what I was told was beautiful was always *hapa* (Hawaiian for "half"), girls who were mixed with white and Asian or Polynesian. Their beauty was heightened and celebrated because of their closeness to whiteness. They were a mixed plate of the familiar (white) and the exotic (Hawaiian or Asian). Though I was also mixed, my blackness didn't garner the same celebration as whiteness. Black womanhood was not centered or celebrated in Hawaii. As in the rest of the United States, we were all but invisible except for tokenized consumption in film, television, and music.

When I left Hawaii, I was excited by the fact that I was entering a space where my being trans was not known by those around me. It would no longer lead the way. And this was freeing, allowing me to be just another girl in the crowd, another twenty-year-old studying and hanging out. I came to Rhode Island confident in the way I presented myself. I was young, stylish, curly, and curvy and had a wide, broad, straight smile. Sure, I had qualms about the fact that my thighs touched, but beyond that, I was secure in my looks. However, I did not calculate the impact of being a black woman in social spaces that valued the white male gaze.

No matter how moisturized my curls, how tight my body, how bright my smile, I was largely overlooked in a racist, patriarchal culture that placed the beauty of thin, white, blond women on a pedestal. Whoever was closest to that ideal was seen and sought. All others were ignored.

At that party, I had my first experience of being both invisible and hypervisible. I was standing in a corner in the living room, listening to the girls discussing *The Bachelor*, a show I believed was the TV equivalent of the "most segregated hour" in America. I knew no black people who watched the dating show. This was more than a decade before ABC casted its first black Bachelorette in 2017. Sam and her friends were split over whether they found the current bachelor, Bob Guiney, cute or not. Sam thought he was an everyman, while most of the girls thought he was too pudgy. I was about to contribute that his curls were obsessively gelled, when this Hulk-like figure wrapped his overbearing arm around Sam's roommate.

"You gonna introduce me or what?" he asked, feigning outrage.

"Tony," Sam's roommate said, rolling her eyes and laughing, "these are my friends."

"Hi, friends," Tony said, waving.

Tony, who had apparently played five too many unsanitary rounds of beer pong, smiled at all the girls before setting his attention on me. With his fixed eyes, he returned to Sam's roommate, whispering loudly in her ear.

"Tony wants to say hi," she said, shrugging her shoulders.

He creepily twiddled his fingers. He was expecting my amusement, but I was bad at concealing my irritation. He was an entitled jock at ease with inserting himself into a group of women—and centering himself. His gaze was unlike anything I had felt before (and this was a lot coming from a woman who had negotiated with and navigated horny men for most of her adolescence). I am not inherently afraid of men, but there was something about the way he was intent on interacting with me that I found unsettling. Still, I extended my hand to shake his, and he met it with his lips. This caused the girls around me to giggle and the guys surrounding us to stare. I was on display, with Tony's public courting taking center stage. I was the exotic creature who had been invisible until this white guy validated my existence. Now I was worthy of being seen.

I pulled my hand back and joined the giggling chorus to defuse the situation. I hoped to laugh off the awkwardness. He detached his biceps from around the shoulders of our mutual acquaintance and moved toward me.

"I didn't get your name," Tony said.

"You never asked," I said, taking a swig from my cup.

"You're tough, *girlfriend*." He moved his head from side to side as if he were imitating *Martin*'s Sheneneh Jenkins.

"Janet," I said, extending my hand again to maintain the distance between us. He grabbed my hand and pulled me to him. He smelled like a musty locker room Febrezed with Dolce & Gabbana Light Blue and beer.

"Janet, can I ask you a personal question?"

I nodded.

"You're striking. What are you?"

"A student," I said.

"Ha! Ha!" he shouted. "Where are you from?"

"Hawaii."

"You're my first Hawaiian," he said, winking. "Damn, is that how you get that glow?"

I laughed, sought refuge in my cup, and pulled myself closer to Sam, who I could feel was uneasy about the interaction.

"Do you hula?" Tony asked. He swayed his stiff hips and extended his arms from side to side like a tourist at a tacky luau.

"No," I lied. I knew that if I said yes, he'd request that I dance for him.

"For real, this girl's skin is unreal. It's like toffee," he said, looking me up and down. "You're fine as hell!"

"OK, that's enough, Tony." It was Jared, the guy from marketing. "Shrek isn't bothering you, is he?"

My heart raced seeing my crush this close. We had never spoken before in class, but I couldn't hide how grateful I was to him for interrupting.

"Man, I'm not bothering anyone," Tony said. "Right, girls?"

"No, you're fine," Sam said.

I believed that no man would want me—if he knew. So for Troy to know and remain was a personal victory. A white cis man, who was taught that he should seek partnership with a white cis woman, choosing me felt transgressive. Our relationship was a resounding *fuck you* to the systems of desire embedded in us.

I was the product of such a relationship. My mother, a Native Hawaiian and Portuguese woman, and my father, a black man from Texas, crossed boundaries of their own when they married in 1982, a year before I was born. My mother was taught by her Native Hawaiian mother to be suspicious of whiteness. It made sense having grown up in Hawaii, a land that was colonized and occupied by the U.S. military, as well as the tourist and agricultural industries. Her mother told her that they were poor, that though she and her mother and her mother before her were born on this land, they had no land of their own because of the white man's grasp and greed. All the white man did was steal and conquer, she learned.

Mom would never desire, love, or bring home a white person. Neither would her five younger siblings. This was a clear family boundary. So when she finally brought a man home—a Southern man whose deep brown skin sparkled in his white Navy uniform like a penny in the sun—she was giddy. My grandmother welcomed Dad with an easy smile, open arms, and a home-cooked meal of garlic chicken, long rice, and Portuguese bean soup. My grandfather, a Portuguese man who drove a street sweeper and worshipped football, sulked into his frosted glass of beer.

Papa's discomfort was natural. It stemmed from paternal protectiveness birthed out of his belief that no one would be good enough for *his* Elizabeth. She was his firstborn—the only one of his six children to mirror his own face back to him with those round brown eyes, that slender pointed nose, and those inelegantly large ears. He brooded as he ate, which soured the meal his wife had made. He was rigid, unable to hear his soon-to-be son-in-law. Papa's coldness never thawed, and my mother internalized his disapproval as her own per-

sonal failure. But my grandfather was not upset with my mother. He was upset with himself for never considering blackness.

As much as they discussed the wrongdoings of powerful white people, my grandparents never discussed black people at home in Kalihi, where African-Americans were rarely seen. Hawaii was a world away from the civil rights movement broadcast on TV screens in my mother's 1960s childhood. Anti-black racism was a mainland ill, not a local issue, Papa thought. He convinced himself that he could *never* behave like those spiteful white men. He could *never* yell at or beat or reject anyone based on their skin color. Papa, who resembled the white man his Portuguese mother briefly dated, served in the Korean War alongside black Marines. He even married a woman who was similarly hued to my own father. But Papa could not help but look at the young black man in the starched dress whites, the one flashing the easy smile, with suspicion. He would not boast about his prejudice or engage with it. He remained silent about his discomfort with my father's blackness. Papa's silence stood in judgment—consistent and covert—throughout my parents' brief marriage.

TROY BROUGHT ME HOME to Maryland in October. He had spent the past month on leave with his family before reporting to the ship in San Diego. When he told me over the phone one night that he wanted me to meet his family, I was nervous about making a good impression. I wanted them—especially his mother—to like me. When we lived together in Hawaii, his mother called at least once a week. They were close, and he always wanted to make her proud. That's probably why he never told her the woman he loved was trans. I appreciated that he was protective of me and my story. I was also too self-conscious about my trans-ness to want anyone I did not know to know. We had an unspoken agreement that the particulars of my journey would remain between us.

New England looked best in early fall, and I basked in its splendor during the five-hour train ride south from Providence to Baltimore. The coasts and bridges sparkled in the morning light. The trees looked like they had been set on fire by the sun. The landscape was painted in ambers and yellows and oranges. I was anxious to see Troy, and the anticipation of our reunion filled my belly with butterflies and doubt. I wondered if he would still think I was worthy of him, his life, his family. When I got off the train, Troy was standing on the platform, with his sly smile and his arms stretched wide open. His warm, enthusiastic kiss built my confidence that he would make our relationship work despite the distance. Nothing had changed, I told myself.

The first person I met in Troy's family was his stepfather, Alan, the man who raised him. He was a self-proclaimed redneck, with a long beard, a Southern accent, and an impressive beer gut. Initially, I was intimidated by his presence, but he was sweet and funny, and his charm made you forget that he reeked of body odor, beer, and chewing tobacco. Alan clashed with the impeccable decor of the four-bedroom home designed by his wife, Linda, who never left the marble counters of her newly renovated kitchen. Linda was Italian, with dark auburn hair that she gathered with a pencil into a sloppy yet chic updo. Everything she did seemed effortless yet was, in reality, perfectly tailored and designed. She worked as a buyer at a high-end home-furnishings store and was an interior design expert. Because of her immaculate home, I thought Troy came from money. He made it plain that this was not his childhood home. He told me he had grown up in a town house without a backyard, just across the street from his school.

His mother had lived all her adult life surrounded by men, two of whom she raised with Alan. She wasn't one of those women who reigned as queen of the castle. Instead, she found it difficult navigating a testosterone-filled home, where the men in her life expected her not only to work all day but also to come home to cook and clean for them. Throughout his adolescence, Troy was her sole ally, the man who seemed to recognize how hard she worked. He most often lent a hand with household chores. She was smitten with her son.

"He was always my little helper, my good boy," she told me over chardonnay. "But once he graduated, he just didn't know what to do with himself when football was over."

She seemed to thrive on the presence of another woman in her house. She spoke openly in essay length about all things Troy, and I was a captive audience with a hungry ear. It was nice to learn more about him. He was not talkative or forthcoming. He felt the past was the past and there was no need to dwell on things you couldn't change.

"He just didn't have a plan," Linda continued. "It was football or nothing. He sat around in the basement, smoking pot and playing video games."

"Hey, woman," Troy called from the living room. "I had a job. Don't make it sound like I was some loser."

"Oh, I know, hon," Linda cooed from the kitchen, before she turned back to me. "Anyway, I know he was just pacifying himself with pot. He wanted to numb himself from being *depressed.*"

She whispered *depressed* like a murmur, a sort of sigh.

"My poor guy was just sad all the time. He tried to pretend around his friends, but they were not doing anything with their lives, you know? And I saw Troy becoming just like them. And it made me so sad, *Janet.*"

The way she said my name made me feel like I was her confidante, as if she were letting me in on family secrets. Troy was her golden boy. It upset her to see him becoming rudderless, heading nowhere at age twenty.

"I've never been one of those overbearing mothers," she said. "But seeing Troy sitting in that basement all day woke me up. It was now or never. So one day I just got tough with him. I told him, 'Troy you have to *do* something with your life or you can't live here anymore. I can't support your deterioration.' And he didn't even look at me when I was talking to him. He just played that damn game."

"He was somewhere else, completely checked out, and as a mom, I felt like I failed him, you know."

I didn't know *that* Troy, the depressed pothead playing video games. I had met the Troy who was set on seeing the world. But Linda's plea worked. After two aimless years, he walked into the Navy recruitment office across the street from the mall and signed himself up for service.

"I want to get out of here," he said, as he completed his application. He came home a few days later with orders to report to boot camp in Alabama.

Linda and I talked the rest of that weekend away, listening to Michael Bublé, drinking white wine, and munching on all the goodies she couldn't stop preparing, from deviled eggs to lasagna. Our most tender moment came a few glasses of wine after our first dinner.

"When I saw that photo of you and Troy at the beach, I knew you were special," she told me, reaching her hand across the Carrara marble to touch mine. "I could never get Troy out of his shirt. He always felt self-conscious about his body, and he probably gets that from me, always talking about my weight like I do. Anyway, when I saw that photo of you two on the beach and he had his shirt off—*with a tan*—I cried. I really did."

As I gathered my things in the guest room on Sunday, I felt accomplished, having spent time with his family, meeting the guys he grew up with, and receiving acknowledgment from his mother for being the catalyst for Troy's bare-chest breakthrough. After brunch, the plan was for Troy to drive me to Rhode Island and spend a few nights with me and my new friends. Our plan took a detour when I picked up the phone in the guest room.

"I can't wait to see you," I heard a woman say.

"Well, I would come out there today, but I have a friend visiting," Troy said.

I slammed the receiver and paced the room. There was a familiarity, an intimacy, in the cadences of their voices. I felt as if I were eavesdropping on a conversation between a couple. It was the kind of call you make with someone you see every day, the kind of call you make with a partner about dinner plans.

A friend? I said to myself. *Is that all I am to him?*

I began sobbing as he walked into the room. He bowed his head.

"A *friend*, Troy?" I pleaded. I was too stunned to be angry. I was overcome by what felt like betrayal. "So all this time you've been talking to some other woman?"

He kept his head bowed and offered no answers as I pelted him with questions. I was in distress.

"Who is she? *Who is she?*"

He didn't look at me. He didn't speak. It seemed as if he were repenting, but I would later learn that he was retreating into himself. He avoided conflict by detaching and disconnecting.

"If you want her, then go be with her!" I screamed, unconcerned that anyone could hear me. "I won't stand in your way."

He didn't answer me. He just left the room. I exhausted myself by crying and retracing our year together, asking myself questions: *Did I make up this relationship? Am I in this alone? Has he been seeing other people this entire time?*

An hour later, I heard a knock on the door. It was Linda.

"Troy went to the store for me," she said. "Come up and have some wine."

For Linda, wine cured all wounds, and I was her patient.

"Tell me what happened," she said, sliding a generously poured glass to me.

"He's seeing someone else," I said, trying my best not to restart the waterworks. "I don't know who she is."

"Eva," she said. "Her name is Eva. They went to school together. They weren't boyfriend and girlfriend, but she was around. I don't think you should be worried about her. She has a child." Then she continued in a whisper, "And the fattest ass I've ever seen. It's quite obscene."

This last detail did not put me at ease. I only felt more threatened.

"I am not your mother, so take what I say with a grain of salt," Linda said, "but I know my son, and he loves *you*, Janet. And I believe you know that. Troy has never brought a girl home, and you are here."

It sounded right and good, and it felt nice. But I was still shaken. Troy had become my foundation. I had grown to depend on him in ways I had never depended on my own parents. He had become my first refuge, the first place I could rest and actually exhale.

I wanted to move on from the anguish and forget the betrayal, so I let Troy drive me to campus, but I did not invite him to stay. When I hugged him good-bye, he looked like any other man to me. This made me feel utterly alone.

SIX

JUST AS QUICKLY AS SOMEONE ENTERS, they can leave. People make mistakes. They disappoint. And you're left with yourself. Being alone is unbearable when you've enjoyed a reprieve with togetherness. I believed in the power of companionship. What I did not know then was that no one can heal you. You must learn to be your own company, your own cure. You cannot retreat into someone else for fulfillment.

Troy's calls, something I used to schedule my day around, now felt like a chore. He begged me for forgiveness. He tried to convince me that Eva meant nothing. He pleaded with me to let him visit me on campus before he flew to San Diego. I didn't let him come. It was difficult to remain a believer in us. Still, I stayed with Troy *and* left Troy. I was unwilling to leave completely, because I didn't want to return to myself.

Cutting ties felt like too harsh a punishment for a phone call. It wasn't as if I had caught him holding on to her plump derriere for dear life. Still, it felt like a betrayal, and I didn't have the experience, the patience, or the maturity to work with Troy to build back the trust. All I knew was that I loved him and he had wronged me. I didn't want to do the emotional labor of facing the incongruity of these truths. I wished I could reach for next-level spiritual goals, like being "able to be alone, to find it nourishing—not just a waiting," as Susan Sontag wrote. I didn't wait, though. I sought and chased warmth in other bodies. I was always reaching for bodies to steady me, to brace myself against. Often because I was bored. Sometimes to fight loneliness. Always because I wanted to get out of my own.

There was Anthony, the Cape Verdean basketball player, whom I began making out with in the library. We'd meet up in a private study room he reserved on Wednesdays after our economics class. For the first fifteen minutes, we would compare lecture notes, before finding a way to each other's body. We'd dry hump to the point of Anthony begging to "put it in." That always signaled my exit.

There was Drew, the dreadlocked resident adviser who lived across the hall from me. He was a convenient companion on nights when I had nothing else to do. We'd smoke out to the point of absolute relaxation. I let him rest his face between my thighs a few times until I was relished to slumber. Sex finally felt *fun*. We explored, we teased, we chased. It wasn't deep. We weren't looking to fall in love. We were looking to feel good, no matter how fleeting the feeling. For years, men had enjoyed my body before I enjoyed *being* in my body. I felt liberated in knowing that my body was capable of not only giving but also accepting pleasure.

Then there was Jared, the handsome football player with the Roman nose in marketing. We played coy since the first class, staring at each other as our professor lectured. An exchange of glances signaled my fall into a deep well of infatuation.

By the end of October, the campus began to chill, and I was in denial about the incoming New England winter, my very first. My wardrobe of deep-cut sweaters, skirts, and tights no longer kept me warm, and I refused to invest in the same L.L. Bean down coat seen all over campus. With its puffy silhouette and below-the-knee hem, the coat made every woman look like a walking overstuffed burrito. I resisted joining the ill-shaped masses in my lightweight H&M parka, which always let the cold in but hit me in all the right places.

I was making my way into marketing class when Jared approached me with a smile. He was breaking the rules of our silent courtship built on stares.

"What are you doing after class?" he asked.

"Going to the dining hall for breakfast," I said.

"Let me take you to breakfast," he said, opening the door.

After class, we rode in his black Range Rover to a diner a few miles from campus. It was one of those restaurants with polished metal covering every surface, the kind of place that looked like it belonged off the side of a New Jersey highway. The diner had just finished serving the morning rush and was settling into a hush. The only sound was running water, popping grease, and clinking silverware. We used our menus to escape the awkwardness of being alone in each other's company for the first time. I ordered pancakes and bacon, and Jared got a spinach omelet with home fries. As we waited for our food, he broke the ice.

"Are you aware that many of my teammates have crushes on you?"

"I am not," I said, sipping my coffee. "But I demand to hear all about it!"

He laughed at this. I never imagined that boys, no less jocks, would talk about me in the locker room. I tried my best to conceal how flattered the thirsty high school girl in me was.

"No one knows your name, so they call you the Hawaiian."

"You know my name. Why didn't you correct them?"

"I didn't want them to know that I was eavesdropping."

"How do they know I'm from Hawaii?"

"Word spreads fast," he said.

The waiter dropped off our plates, and I began to butter my pancakes as he cut into his food.

"So what made you ask me out?" I said.

"Your eyes," he said. "No one's stared at me the way you do. You're pretty intense."

I knew then that I would sleep with Jared. He paid the check and invited me to chill at his place. When we walked into his house, I was surprised by how clean it was. I had only ever seen it filled with people, smelling of beer and perspiration.

"Can I get you something to drink?"

"Water's good," I said.

I stood in the living room awkwardly while Jared fussed about in the kitchen. He returned with two glasses of water and invited me to sit on the couch. We had just spent the last two hours together, sharing all that two strangers can share through conversation. So we reverted to locking eyes, and he leaned over and kissed me. He pushed his face into my neck, tickling it with the rough stubble of his short beard. I leaned into him and fell back into the couch. We were feeling and grabbing and unbuttoning, and then the front door opened.

A short bald guy with a backpack revealed himself as we peeled away from each other and tidied ourselves.

"Sorry, man," the intruder said sheepishly.

"It's OK," Jared said, adjusting himself. "Pete, this is Janet. Janet, Pete."

Pete waved, and I was too embarrassed to do anything but smile.

"All right," Pete said. "I'll leave you to it."

Pete went into his bedroom, and Jared grabbed my hand.

"I'm so sorry," he said.

"Don't worry about it," I said. "It's not a big deal."

"No, not about Pete," he said, rubbing his other hand through his hair. "I should've told you that I have a girlfriend."

"Oh," I said, taken aback by his revelation.

"I hope you're not mad. It's just that I haven't ever been attracted to someone as much as I am to you, and I tried to keep my distance, but I just couldn't."

Despite the flattery, my ego was bruised. My imaginings of us going back to that diner and making it our thing vanished. I couldn't play the role of outraged woman, though. I, too, had kept someone secret.

"I'm fine, really," I said. "I have a complicated relationship of my own, so I can't really fault you for not saying something sooner."

"We're cool?"

"Totally."

When he dropped me off at my apartment, he leaned over to kiss me on the cheek and met the left corner of my bottom lip. I knew we weren't done.

The next time I saw him, we were stealing kisses in his kitchen during a party a few weeks later. He tasted like vodka with a splash of lust.

"Fuuuuuck," he whispered. "Why are you doing this to me?"

"Doing what?"

"You're here at my party, but you're not here with me."

"You have a girlfriend, Jared," I scolded.

"I know. I know. I know," he said. "Still . . ."

Though I wanted to sleep with Jared, I was convinced I shouldn't. The prelude to sex was always more fun than actual penetration. I didn't want to give up on this simmering flirtation. I might not have been old enough to legally consume those cranberry vodkas, but I had lived long enough to know that being someone's side chick wasn't something I ever wanted on my romantic résumé. It triggered me in too many ways: the secret part, the second-fiddle-to-a-white-girl part, the black-girl-mistress part.

"Stay with me tonight," Jared pleaded in my ear.

"You're drunk," I said.

"No, I'm not," he said, pulling himself upright into an impeccable posture. "I just want you around. *Stay with me.*"

He looked so damn cute, begging me like that. Besides, what waited for me at home? A wine-drunk Irishwoman and my empty bed? I was upset with myself for giving in so easily. Lust and infatuation and temptation could talk you into nearly anything. I embraced the sweet delusion that ignited all affairs: *This time, it will be different.*

As the crowd dispersed to their dorms, I helped Jared and his roommates pick up the cups and cans that littered the house. My high-heeled booties clung to the hardwood floors, sticky with spilled booze. When they retired to their rooms, Jared and I enjoyed the crisp air on the back patio, which was lit by the glow of clear twinkling lights. We shared a blanket on a chaise lounge and leaned into each other. He kissed me as if he were in pursuit of something. He was slow and purposeful in his quest.

His palm slid down my chest, down my belly, and into the front of my jeans. He didn't bother to unbutton or unzip me. He pressed the top of his palm right where my body pulsed. I grabbed his hand and whispered for him to come inside. We clumsily wriggled out of our jeans, and I pulled his shirt off. His torso was sculpted, with smooth, taut, tan skin. I grabbed his hips and pulled him toward me. I kissed and licked his stomach before freeing him from his briefs. He found warmth in my mouth. After a few minutes, his fingers curled under my chin, and he lifted my face to meet his in a kiss. He pushed me gently with the weight of his body onto my back. He looked me in the eyes as if to ask if this was OK, and I gripped him in response. He put on a condom, and I guided him into me. Eventually, he took over, until I whimpered little cries that met his groans in a crescendo all our own.

It was the culmination of a sweet courtship, one that ended in the harshness of the morning sun, where he greeted me with a kiss. We engaged in postcoital pleasantries, sharing eggs, coffee, and a shower. He dropped me off at my apartment and searched my face for answers. I burrowed my face in his neck to avoid his eager eyes.

A FEW DAYS LATER, Troy called from San Diego to check in. He spoke in a fast-paced manner that seemed out of character. He relayed details about his new apartment (a condo in Mission Valley), his new truck (a 2003 Toyota Tundra), and his new workplace (an aircraft carrier stationed on picturesque Coronado Island). He seemed genuinely happy, which made me bitter. It wasn't that I didn't want him to be happy; I just didn't want him to be happy without me. Petty, I know.

"You've gotta come here. It's beautiful!" he said. "Will you come for Thanksgiving?"

"I can't," I said, unmoved. "I'm going to New York that weekend."

Anytime he brought up the possibility of making holiday plans, I was noncommittal. I emotionally manipulated Troy as punishment for a phone call, which was damn near virginal considering the series of hookups I had poured myself into after that initial betrayal. It's not even fair to say that the phone call prompted me into the beds of other men. It just gave me license to act on flirtations that had long simmered.

Troy was eager for my affirmation and believed that being a steady presence would win out in the end. He was confident that I would come to my senses, forgive and forget. Still, no man could get between New York City and me. My friend Leo had invited me to join him and his family's annual Thanksgiving weekend shopping trip in the city, and I couldn't have wished for a better invitation.

I had been lazily running laps on the school's indoor track at the recreation center when I first crossed paths with Leo. He was leading rehearsals with his dance troupe, perfecting choreography to the just-released Britney Spears song, "(I Got That) Boom Boom," a collaboration with the Ying Yang Twins. Their precision made me stop in my tracks, ditching my half-hearted workout attempt. I sat and watched them for a half hour. I loved how kind yet exacting Leo was with his dancers. I found this quality admirable, and it propelled me to introduce myself to him. We became fast friends, bonding over our love of Janet Jackson and *Ally McBeal* and our dreams of conquering New York City—the only way two people in their twenties truly believe they can.

Leo was a proud Italian-American boy from Connecticut. He was fit, tan, and impeccably groomed. In all the years I've known him, I've never seen him without his hair blown out and gelled to perfection. I've always admired that he is unapologetic about the effort it takes to look good. But he was more than just a pretty face. He was a full-time student who flipped houses with his father. He had a close-knit family that he visited every free weekend he got. I could not understand why a young person would feel so compelled to be pulled home.

I was living a continent away from my own family, hadn't seen my father since I was twelve, and was completely OK with being on a different coast from my first love. I was not pining for anyone. Sometimes I wondered if I had some kind of intimacy disorder, if I had inherited something from my rolling-stone father, who never seemed to settle or attach himself to any one person, even his own children. There were moments when I felt lonely and missed genuine connection, the kind I had experienced with my brother Chad when we were kids. I missed being with people with whom I shared continuity. But I think we all crave those spaces, the ones where shared history acts as a thread holding us accountable to our former selves and to one another.

Maybe that's why Leo made that drive on the weekends, to maintain those connections that were so valuable to him. College wasn't forever, the way home was, I guessed. I wondered if I was not pulled home, tethered to one spot, because I hadn't found what home was yet.

Leo's family treated me as if I had always been one of them during that Thanksgiving weekend, like a first cousin who lived out of state. I remember the giddiness I felt when that white stretch limousine pulled into the driveway of their sprawling home. I couldn't believe I was going to New York City, in a damn limo, no less. We piled into the car—me, Leo, his mother, stepfather, little brother, and two stepsiblings. We sipped champagne during our two-hour drive to Manhattan, whose massive profile, lit in a constellation of manmade stars, seemed to ascend through the dark gray clouds seen from my limo window as we crossed the Triborough Bridge. It was a galaxy of its own.

The Marriott Marquis in Times Square was our home for the weekend, but I didn't plan to stay there. It would simply house my belongings, bathe me, give me a place to nap. I couldn't believe the flashing lights, the billboards, the buildings, the crowds, the taxis. I was in the middle of Times Square, a sight I had seen daily after school beamed into my living room on TV. I was standing where Beyoncé, Kelly Rowland, and Michelle Williams had stood. Every picture I had cataloged in my mind growing up came to life that weekend, but New York, I knew, was more than MTV studios, the Virgin Megastore, and Olive Garden. I yearned to see the less telegenic New York, to be part of the real New York.

Leo and I peeled away from his family in the late afternoons, taking a horse-drawn carriage ride in Central Park, eating Magnolia cupcakes in the West Village, posing for fake IDs in a tattoo parlor on MacDougal Street, dipping and doing it in gay bars on and around Christopher Street.

"One belongs to New York instantly, one belongs to it as much in five minutes as in five years," Tom Wolfe wrote. I knew this city was mine. For me, New York was a chalkboard waiting to be filled in. I could erase myself and draw a new existence. The city allowed for anyone to come as they wanted to be. That weekend filled me to the brim with possibility, but I knew ours was more than a two-day affair. I was not through with New York City and vowed to return.

After Thanksgiving break, the campus was covered in snow and went into a lull. If you lived on campus, there were no parties to attend, as students hunkered down for final exams and end-of-term projects and papers. People were also paired up by now, retreating into the comfort of coupledom. Boredom and a lack of companionship led me to message Anthony, my study-and-make-out buddy.

hey! what you doing?

chillin. u?

soooo bored.

come over. hang w me. im fun ;-)

mmmhhhhmmm

not kidding.

all right but no funny business :-P

promise.

I turned off my laptop, fluffed my hair, and put on some blush, mascara, and a spritz of my favorite perfume, Clinique's Happy. Anthony lived in a single room in the dorms across from the dining hall. I had only been to his room once to pick up notes he had taken for an economics lecture I missed.

Anthony was allegedly a star basketball player. I say allegedly because I never attended a game. He must have been pretty good, because he seemed to have a new girl with him every time I saw him in the dining hall. He was very good-looking and knew it, standing at six-foot-four, with light brown skin and hazel eyes. He was the kind of guy I could tolerate only when I was lustful, bored, or both.

I joined him on his gray futon to watch an episode of HBO's *The Wire*. I hadn't given this show the attention it deserved when it originally aired because *Sex and the City* had sucked my energy. I now know that we were watching an episode from the second season, when the show shifted its focus from the projects of Baltimore to the docks.

"I thought this was about drugs," I said.

"It is, but this season, they're trying to make us care about working-class white people."

"I see," I said, uninterested.

"Wanna watch something else?" he asked, extending the remote to me.

When I reached to grab it, he pointed his finger to his cheek. He was an expert flirt, so I kissed him. He handed the remote over. I turned to MTV, where Jessica Simpson was serving dumb-blonde realness for the masses on *Newlyweds*.

"She's intolerable," Anthony said, moving to the floor between my legs. "So dumb!"

"Trust me, she is not dumb," I argued, immediately defensive of my current guilty pleasure and its heroine. "She's *playing* dumb because that is what America expects of women—especially blond white ones. She knows what she is doing."

"I don't think she's *that* subversive," he said, resting his head between my knees.

I could tell he was bored by the mundane lives of the rich and famous, but I continued watching anyway. I loved reality TV's ability to pacify me, to lull me when I needed a reprieve from course work and studying. I rubbed Anthony's head as consolation, the short bristles of his coarse hair scraping my palm. He grabbed my hand and kissed my wrist, leaving goose bumps in the imprint of his wet kiss. I pulled my hand away in an effort to make him pause. He continued anyway, turning around to meet me face-to-face on his knees as I rested on the couch.

I kissed him and patted the spot next to me to direct him to sit and watch TV on the couch. He ignored my signal and placed his hands on my shoulders as a means of holding me in place. He pressed his mouth to my neck, biting me softly below my ear, kissing me right above the collarbone. His face rested between my breasts. I knew these moves; his choreography never changed. In the library, it was easy to withdraw from his advances because it was a public space. In the shadows of his bedroom, he was unstoppable. He stood up and began to slip his sweatpants down. I tried not to roll my eyes in response.

"Come on," I said. "Let's watch TV."

"You didn't come here to watch TV."

"Yes, I did."

"Take your top off."

"I'm leaving," I said, reaching for my sweater on the couch next to me.

"No, you're not," he snapped, snatching my sweater, which he draped over his wide shoulders. "If you want it, come get it."

I stood to grab it, and he pushed me with little effort back to the spot I had risen from. "Stop it," I said. "This isn't funny!"

He chuckled and tossed my sweater across the room, where it landed on his bed. I rolled my eyes in exasperation. This time, he let me stand up. I pushed him out of my way and retrieved my sweater. He trailed me and pushed me onto the bed. I landed on my belly. When I turned toward him, his dick was in his hand, held up by the tension in the tight elastic waistband of his gray sweats. He began to stroke himself.

"OK, I'm leaving *for real* now," I said, attempting to get up.

Anthony fell onto the bed, pushing me onto my back. He rose to his knees and straddled me while stroking himself rigorously.

"Take off your pants," he said.

"No," I rolled my eyes. "Just finish yourself off."

"I said, take off your pants."

"No!"

He stopped stroking himself. He put both hands on my waist. I gripped the elastic band of my tights to keep them up.

"I'm taking them off," he said.

I understood then that consent for him was not me expressing my desire to have sex. He felt he *deserved* to have my body because I had come to his room and he desired me. Walking past the threshold of his room was consent enough. Having made out with him before was consent enough. Being forced into a corner so I had no choice but to yield was consent enough. Saying yes or no didn't matter.

He forced my tights down and pulled my thong to the side to enter me. He kept pushing despite the fact that I squeezed him with my thighs, despite the friction and the tightness, despite the fact that I turned my face away, despite the fact that I cried for him to stop, to not cum in me. *He can't even do that,* I thought, as he pushed deeper inside me and finished.

I peeled myself away, got dressed, and walked out. I passed the courtyard that separated my apartment from the dining hall and the dorms. The hills were covered with snow that had yet to be touched. It was pristine, the kind of white that reflects light even in the deepest of night. Three girls, bundled in parkas with matching fur-lined hoods, stood atop one of the hills. They were holding dining trays in their gloved hands. One of the girls was shaking her furry head, and I could hear her friends squealing a pep talk: "It's gonna be fun!" "Don't be scared!" "Trust us!" "Come on!"

As I turned the key to my room, the girls' screams and cackles pierced my frozen ears. I washed the night off me and wondered if the girl fought her reluctance and took the joy ride. I felt silly for caring, so I made a sobbing noise, trying to force a cry. Tears didn't come.

SEVEN

THE REMNANTS OF THAT NIGHT never left me. By instinct, my thighs tightened for years every time a man hovered over me. To this day, anytime I pass a fragrance counter or a woman wearing Happy, I am taken right back to that bed on that snowy night. Anthony stripped me of the comfort I was just beginning to enjoy in my body. He reminded me—someone who had grown up with the Spice Girls and Destiny's Child chanting "Girl Power" and "Independent Women"— that no matter how empowered I felt, I could still be disempowered, made small and vulnerable. My body, no matter how much I grew to accept it, could be violated. No matter how much I learned to embrace it, it couldn't always protect me from unyielding force.

We have continuity in our bodies, which hold experiences that never leave us, experiences our bodies conceal so we can keep going. They hold tightly to them—until we have confidence to trust our bodies again, to loosen their grasp. This relaxation never came to me. My body did not rest. It did not yield. It remained clenched for nearly all of my twenties.

Every once in a while, regret surfaced in the form of what-ifs and the dozens of different things I *should've* done. I blamed myself for leaving him with blue balls all those times in the library. I blamed myself for being so needy, for seeking the company of another that night. I blamed myself for being too cheeky, too familiar, too comfortable. I blamed myself for not saying *no* loudly enough, for not deepening my voice in a commanding way. I blamed myself for pursuing my sweater on his bed. I blamed myself for not screaming, scratching, punching, kicking, *resisting*.

This ceaseless soliloquy made sleep impossible. Those last weeks in Rhode Island were a blur of lectures and cram sessions, fake smiles and nods, meals and dreamless nights. I backed out of group dinners and movie dates, blaming it all on finals and term papers. I retreated to long, hot, pitch-black showers, crying into the darkness, wringing myself out. It was the only thing that made me feel OK, clearing and uncluttering my mind. In the midst of this clarity, I called Troy in a murmur, forming my voice in a way that opened him up to me.

"Troy?" I wept into my phone. I was sitting on the edge of the tub as steam moved around me.

"What's wrong?" he asked, concerned.

"I have to tell you something."

"OK."

"I slept with someone else."

He let out a soul-crushing sob. I had never heard a sound so heartbreaking. I sat on the phone and listened to him bawl. I felt for him, but this was exactly what I wanted. I wanted to be heard, but I also wanted someone, anyone, to hurt as much as I was hurting. I aimed to control him because I did not have control over anything else.

"I am sorry," I said. "Forgive me."

I was hustling him into heartbreak that I hoped would curdle into rage. I wanted him to yell at me, to curse me, to dismiss me. But I could not make Troy hate me, no matter how hard I tried. He did not leave me. He told me to come to him, and I did. I spent the winter break with him. His forgiving embrace felt like home, like comfort. *These arms will not hurt me*, I told myself. I held tightly to Troy, because as long as I was with him, I felt I would not be violated again. I'd be protected, because I was someone, a woman, who now belonged to someone, a man.

He wanted to forget and to erase. He made me believe that I was worthy of another chance, a fresh start. I vowed not to leave him, and I never returned to Rhode Island, though I remained friends with both Leo and Sam. I stayed by Troy's side as he prepared to set out to sea. We rebuilt what we had neglected by being together every day those next five months. We ate and slept, cooked and cleaned, kissed and cuddled, teased and tickled, laughed and came . . . and all of a sudden, grudges gave way to forgiveness, and pain subsided into healing. All of a sudden, I felt all right and safe and unbroken. It wasn't an *Aha!* that I could pinpoint; it was a feeling that emerged through the quiet process of silencing and deleting and choosing to live.

A week before Troy was deployed, I made him see *Mean Girls* with me for the third time at Fashion Valley Mall. It was the only thing that delayed the oncoming melancholy of our inevitable parting. We were driving to our favorite Mexican restaurant, which served super-sized crunchy ground-beef tacos (that I still dream about), when he turned toward me with a proposal.

"I think we should get married," he said.

"What?"

"Hear me out. I've been thinking about this," he said. "If we got married, you wouldn't have to get a job when you go back to school. You could concentrate on getting your degree. The quicker you graduate, the faster you can be back here with me."

I knew the military compensated married active-duty members, enabling them to care for their dependents, especially when deployed. His was a down-to-earth proposal, a financial solution that would enable him to provide for me when I returned to Hawaii to complete my final three semesters of undergrad. I was moved, not by the romance of a man choosing me but by the practicality of his love. He was concerned with my well-being in a way no one else had been. My parents hadn't been prepared to have children. They had been Troy's age when I came into their lives. I never doubted their love for me, but they were young and messy, preoccupied with the parts they played in their own love story.

My love story with Troy was barely two years old. We had never talked about marriage, though we did talk about the future. Of course, I had let myself daydream about walking down the aisle, but I never thought that was a real possibility. I grew up in a world where girls like myself rarely got the guy, where partnership wasn't readily accessible, safety wasn't guaranteed, and love wasn't part of the equation. None of the girls I had grown up with had long-term partners. I had no blueprint for happily ever after. But here was a man I loved, who accepted me for who I was, who had forgiven my wrongs, who most often did right by me, who was telling me that he wanted to make me his wife and take care of me.

I didn't know if it was the right answer, but it felt right when I said "I do" later that week at the San Diego County Clerk's office. I wore a blue maxi dress, the only long garment I owned. He wore a white shirt and gray pants. It was just the two of us (no family or friends were present); two employees led our ceremony and served as our witnesses. We kissed overlooking a gleaming marina. We didn't exchange rings, but he surprised me with a white iBook with a Post-it quoting his favorite Dave Matthews song: *I remember thinking I'll go on forever only knowing I'll see you again.*

He cried and clutched my waist in bed that night. His face pressing into my belly, he kept telling me that he was sorry and that he loved me. I cried with him, craving to know what he was sorry about. I didn't ask, though—too afraid he'd say he didn't really want to marry me, that he had regrets. I steadily stroked his blond head, hoping to brush away any doubt that lingered.

We wouldn't share a bed for another six months, and I returned to

Oahu. I jumped right into summer school, taking a semester's worth of classes in two back-to-back six-week summer sessions. I was determined to graduate with my class and return to Troy in Southern California after commencement. Troy, who worked in the captain's office on the ship, wrote to me almost daily, telling me about the overseas ports he visited, from Japan and Malaysia to Australia and the United Emirates. I was elated that he was finally seeing the world. The promise of travel had lured him to the Navy. He ended every email telling me he wished I were there with him. We were far apart but had never been closer. He was a constant presence through correspondence, and it was the crafting of those emails that reconnected me to my love of the written word. I was my best in words—clear and secure in what I felt, what I believed, who I was. As Joan Didion said, "I write entirely to find out what I'm thinking, what I'm looking at, what I see and what it means. What I want and what I fear."

THAT FALL, I SIGNED up for a journalism course and began writing for the daily student newspaper, *Ka Leo O Hawaii*, where I reported as a features writer. I had always loved books—a pastime I inherited from my mother, a woman who read *everything*, from Stephen King and Jackie Collins to Louisa May Alcott and Jane Austen. She loved mysteries and lived for drama, enabling her to fade away momentarily into the entanglements of others. Mom took me to get my first library card when I was twelve, and it was among those stacks that I began to see possibilities for what my life could be in the bound pages of books.

I imagined myself writing books someday but never thought I could support myself doing that. It didn't seem practical for someone who didn't have a financial safety net to sit, think, and put words to paper. *Who wants to hear from me, anyway?* I asked myself. As a first-generation college student, acutely aware that I could only afford university because philanthropists had paid my way, I attended college not merely to find my passion and learn but also out of necessity. I needed to find a way to make money, to support myself, to build a career, so I wouldn't be forced to live from paycheck to paycheck like my mother or rely on social safety nets like my father, a veteran who collected disability checks.

Journalism became a way for me to combine my passion for the written word with my need to make a living. It was in Journalism 101—an immersive course that would train future journalists in the age of "new media," a trendy euphemism for digital, Internet, anything beyond traditional print and television—that I made my start and was truly tested for the first time academically. The program was led by Dr. Beverly Keever, a hard-nosed reporter turned academic who had covered the Vietnam War for *Newsweek,* the *New York Herald Tribune,* and the *Christian Science Monitor.* Her work in Vietnam had earned her a Pulitzer Prize nomination. She was the real deal and cared about the craft of reporting and writing. She didn't like fluff, especially the articles I was writing for the daily student paper, including trend pieces ("Graphic Tees Help Students Make Statements") and feel-good profiles of campus figures such as a librarian janitor who was an undocumented poet from South America.

As a young writer, I was ageist toward Dr. Keever, thinking she was too old-school, stringent, and stuck in her ways. It was easier for me to dismiss her than to actually do it her way, which was the hard and right way. Initially, I was a lazy reporter. I didn't really want to report so much as I felt I had something to say and loved interviewing people—not so much about policy but about their lives. I didn't realize then how they intersected.

Despite my arrogance, Dr. Keever encouraged me by showing me that even pop culture and fashion fluff required solid reporting, deep research, and a keen eye for detail. She stayed with me long after her scheduled office hours and gave me notes, made suggestions about potential interviews, and line-edited my work, which made me a much better writer and, more important, a critical thinker. Though I loved the act of sitting with myself and writing, Keever taught me that this work was not a solitary task; it involves collaboration between a writer, her sources, and her editor.

When I wasn't on campus, I enjoyed being home with Mom, Jeff, and Chad, who were happy that Troy was officially a part of our family despite being upset about our elopement. Chad had returned to Hawaii from college in Missouri a few weeks after I did. He loved playing football for Avila College in Kansas City, but the game lost its gleam when there was no one he loved in the audience. My brother was homesick and wanted to play football for the Rainbow Warriors. He fulfilled that dream when he walked on that summer and made the team. My only regret was that I was not able to see my brother play wide receiver because my year at home coincided with the year he was required to sit out because of NCAA transfer requirements.

Mom and Jeff had moved to a condo in Aiea before the holidays, finally leaving Kalihi, our beloved hometown, which had been the site of all my adolescent milestones, from first crushes and best-friendships to prom and graduation. Mom said the neighborhood "wasn't the same," deteriorating due to poverty, gangs, and meth. She retreated to the much safer Honolulu suburb, a few blocks from landmarks like Pearl Harbor and Aloha Stadium, home to the annual NFL Pro Bowl. Now the four of us packed into a two-bedroom in a well-maintained building with an empathetic landlord who ignored Mom's below-average credit score.

We were on the sixth floor, overlooking the lush hillsides of Aiea Heights and Keaiwa Heiau State Park. Mom and I shared the master bedroom, sleeping on a queen bed together, while Chad and Jeff stored their clothes in the smaller bedroom, where Chad slept on Jeff's extra-long twin bed. Jeff, who was addicted to his PlayStation, had no qualms about sleeping on the couch in the living room, where he could stay up late cracking out on *Grand Theft Auto: San Andreas* and *Madden NFL* while listening to Sublime, a recent discovery for a millennial obsessed with alternative skater culture.

No one was more excited to have a full house again than Jeff, who had spent the past two years alone with Mom in a relatively empty and calm apartment—which was out of character for my mother, who seemed to be a magnet for houseguests and chaos. Jeff was sixteen and towering over me at nearly six feet. He was all limbs, with a skater-boy aesthetic and Sun-In orange hair that he shaped into spikes with concrete-like gel. Jeff's hunger for us all to be together—from our morning carpools to our Friday nights filled with Papa John's pizza, *malasadas*, and Blockbuster rentals—distracted me from the fact that Troy was continents away. It was a precious period, when I got a second chance to do the mundane with my family for an extended time.

My mother wasn't the type to dwell on past wrongdoings. She raised my brothers and two older sisters, who had families and homes of their own, to forgive and forget. I tried my best not to dwell on those times in my teenage years when she seemed exclusively committed to Rick, a man lost to crystal meth and drawn to criminal activity. During some of my most turbulent years grappling with my identity and my body, my mother was largely absent. I wanted her to support me, which she did by not getting in my way, but she wasn't *there*. This enabled me to do what I wanted as a young person with a mother who let me lead the way, because she didn't necessarily have answers or solutions to an experience that was unfamiliar territory. Unknowingly, her absence instilled in me a fierce independence, teaching me that my life was mine. I was solely responsible for it.

Mom bounced back from that dark period when her druggie lover was locked up just after my high school graduation in 2001. She found her road to recovery with the help of a megachurch that rented my alma mater's 1,100-seat auditorium for a series of weekend services. We were not raised with religion, so I had always been wary of its place in my life, but I saw what it did for my mother. Her faith, which enabled her to pick up the pieces, heal herself, and speak her desires through the act of prayer, was a courageous act of humility. I admired that she didn't doubt and judge—she *believed*.

Love is also a belief, a leap of faith that you take with someone else, one that is only made all the more perilous with distance. Distance at first feels overwhelming. You cry and miss, and you don't know how you'll cope without your beloved. Then you realize that you can get through a day, then a week, then a month. Routine becomes your savior, enabling you to halt all the missing and to do without. No longer is the person you love integral to your daily survival. You realize you can do it—on your own. Then distance shrinks, and he is in a room with you after six long months, and you have said everything there needs to be said in emails that have acted as glue. Memories of good times together encourage you, and experiences that the other was not part of feel like betrayals. This is what sat between Troy and me after we got over the newness of seeing each other that October when his ship was at Pearl Harbor for a week.

We did not get a hotel room for his weekend in port, because Troy was obsessed with saving money during his deployment. His goal was to have enough for a down payment on a home. He was an American sailor who believed that owning a fraction of his country was the path to building personal wealth. It was something he felt he was promised in exchange for his service. Our living expenses were minimal while Troy was overseas, since my mother thought it offensive to charge her children rent. We were responsible for my summer-school tuition (fall and spring were covered through my merit and Native Hawaiian scholarships), gas for Mom's Mazda, electricity and cable bills. I say all of this to illustrate that we could have afforded a few nights in a Waikiki hotel to have a private space for our reunion. But Troy was adamant during our last call. He was impatient, irritable, and noticeably detached, so I submitted to him, adjusting my tone in a way that signaled that I was a *good wife*.

I wrote off his attitude, blaming stress, distance, and his over-worked, always-on-the-clock schedule, not to mention a lack of daily access to sun and shitty twin bunk beds. But no matter how much I tried to empathize with him, I felt in the deepest part of my gut that it was not justified exhaustion.

My suspicions were confirmed when I greeted him at the dock. He was in his white uniform, complete with matching cotton hat and black neckerchief. I gave him a white puakenikeni and pikake lei, and he kissed me as if he had just seen me yesterday. It was our first time in Hawaii since we had lived here together, so I was determined to create the perfect weekend. I shrugged off his unenthusiastic reception, again blaming it on fatigue. As I drove us to the apartment, I listed all the places we would visit and all the things we'd eat, from Waimea Bay and Lanikai Beach to Matsumoto shave ice, Spam *musubi*, and sushi. Food was always a motivator for Troy, who requested that we head straight to his favorite sushi restaurant.

Troy didn't look well. He was naturally alabaster, with rosy cheeks, but the lack of sun really took all the glow out of him. I still loved his blue eyes and the way the skin around them had matured and creased, making him look less boyish, more rugged. We took a seat at the rotating sushi bar, where little boats floating on water carried our favorites, like *ahi poke*, grilled eel, and *karaage* chicken. He perked up a bit after getting some *poke* in his belly, and I suggested we see a movie after dinner. At this, he shrugged.

"Got any other ideas?" I asked perkily.

"Not really," he said, pouring *shoyu* directly onto his roll. "I'm tired."

"We can always rent a movie," I suggested. "And you can relax."

"That's cool."

When we got to the apartment it was five P.M., and no one had arrived home yet. Troy wasn't too tired to undress me, his eager, rough hands gripping the flesh of my thighs as he held my legs up. We made love feverishly yet quietly under the covers. By the time we showered, everyone was home. Jeff was ecstatic to see Troy, who finally seemed to be present, more like himself. *I knew it was just a phase, I told myself. There's nothing to worry about, Insecure Girl.* They quickly settled in the living room with the PlayStation. He hadn't been near a console in months, so I just rubbed his head and shoulders as he talked shit to Jeff.

Around nine P.M., his phone rang, and he took it on the lanai so as not to disturb Mom, who was in Chad's bedroom reading. From my spot on the couch in the living room, I could hear a high-pitched voice screaming over loud music through Troy's phone.

"Try somewhere on Lewers," he said, referring to a street in Waikiki lined with clubs, bars, and restaurants. "They've got some cool military-friendly spots."

He was quiet for bit, then continued. "Maaaan . . . I can't."

Then he slid the door shut and rolled his eyes in mock irritation toward me. The hairs on my arms stood up, and I tried to listen more intently. All I heard was him repeat, "I can't," which was enough to push me off the couch and onto the lanai.

"Everything OK?" I asked.

He nodded and shooed me with his hand.

You've been here before, I told myself. My heart was beating rapidly, and my feet were itching to walk closer, to shrink the distance. It was always this distance. He was so close but so far away. I wanted to reach out and snatch his phone from his hand.

"Who is that?" I asked, failing at masking my accusatory tone.

He put his phone down toward his thigh.

"It's a couple of my yeomen," he said. "They don't know where to go tonight, and they want me to take them out. I told them I would, but I gotta check with you."

He was awaiting my approval, which he knew was not coming. We had spent six months apart, and on his first night with me, he wanted to spend time with people he'd been on a ship with for the past six months? They were his every day, his constant. They were his people. I was something he maintained, and they were there.

"You're telling me you would rather go to a bar than be here with me?"

"I didn't say that, *Janet*. I am asking if it'd be OK to have a few drinks with my coworkers."

I put my face in my hands.

"You can come, too," he offered, conciliatory. He knew I would not want to hang with his friends. I was hypercritical of anyone who spent more time with Troy than I did. My possessiveness used to be cute to him, but tonight it was poison that disintegrated any warm feelings he may have reserved for me.

"I'll call you back," he said into the phone, the telltale laughter of drunk girls coming through loud and clear from the receiver.

"You take everything so personal," he said.

"How am I supposed to take it? You just got here, and now you want to leave."

"I invited you."

"I don't want to go." I seethed.

"You have not changed. Always so fucking suspicious."

He was direct, hurling judgment without hesitation.

"*Changed?* What fucking changes do you want from me?"

"You know what I meant."

"No, I do not, or I wouldn't have *asked* you."

"This is stupid," he said. "I'm not doing this with you."

"No! I am not doing this with *you*," I said, opening the glass door. "Go spend your time with those giggling whores."

It was an empty command meant to provoke. He didn't have a car; he was too thrifty to rent one or to call a taxi, so he had no way out. He was trapped. He walked off the lanai and returned to the couch. He fixed his face into a smile to face Jeff, grabbed the controller, and spun his index finger around his ear. *Crazy*, he was telling Jeff, who giggled cautiously.

I watched Troy for a while from the lanai and thought about the time he'd told me with a smirk that he never had to approach a woman. At first, I called bullshit, and then I realized that I had never pursued a man before meeting Troy in that club. He had a boyish quality that made me feel self-assured in my sexual aggression. It felt like I could teach him things. My lust for him was clear, which was out of character. I was usually much more cautious and unbothered when it came to men, yet I had still ended up in his bed. He had put minimal effort forward, and I knew that if I had fallen for it, other women had, too. This revelation sowed seeds of uncertainty in me, which soon blossomed into doubt.

EIGHT

SEEING TROY AS HE WAS—NOT AS I WANTED HIM TO BE—had a way of changing my plans. He was no longer my safe haven. I decided I had to take refuge elsewhere. I didn't yet know *where* I would go, but the destination became clearer one day when I was killing time before class.

I was sitting lazily in the sun with Lindsey and Keiko, two journalism classmates I had met in Dr. Keever's class. We were on the grand green staircase at the student union, feeling the honeyed warmth across our shoulders, as Lindsey spoke in the rapid-paced style of a Gilmore Girl.

Lindsey, who had returned to college after taking a few years off to travel, was telling us about one of her far-off adventures (Paris? Barcelona? The Azores?) in which she had flung herself into the arms of some gorgeous (French? Spanish? Portuguese?) man. I couldn't help but be enraptured by her tales of tasting the world. She was a woman free in her wanderings, who recognized that Keiko and I, both local girls, had not traveled.

"You have to promise me you'll go someday. *Promise!*" she said, her brown eyes flecked in gold and as wide as a Bratz doll's. We nodded attentively.

I used the pause in conversation to discuss the possibility of extending my studies by a year in order to declare a double major in journalism and fashion merchandising. I had enough credits to complete my merchandising degree within the year but would need the additional time to concentrate on journalism. I had a clear vision of myself being a features editor at a fashion magazine, likely fueled by depictions of magazine-editor protagonists in *How to Lose a Guy in 10 Days*, *Brown Sugar*, and *13 Going on 30*.

"I wouldn't do that," Lindsey said. She was pulling her silky chestnut hair into a ponytail, which signaled that she meant business.

"Lindsey!" Keiko scolded, smacking her leg. "Don't listen to *her*," she told me. "Do what *you* want!"

Keiko had steely, determined eyes the shapes of shelled pistachios. She stood only three-foot-six, but her personality towered over us, with her cutting wit and strong resolve against the ableist behaviors of those of us who were not little people. I admired her tolerance for the steady stream of pedestrians gawking at her as she navigated campus in her bedazzled kitten heels and silver walker. Instead of hyperventilating in rage like me, Keiko, a Japanese and Korean girl from Kaimuki, would say, "I know what you're thinking, so let's clear this up. The politically correct term is . . . Asian-American."

We grew close over lunch dates of pan-fried noodles, *manapua*, and crispy chicken at McCully Chop Suey—so close that during one of those lunches, I felt safe enough to open up to her. It was her own visible otherness as a person with dwarfism that made me feel confident that she would not judge me. I was sure that disclosing to her would actually bring us closer. Her friendship had become something I valued, and I began to fear that someone would tell her before I could. Over hot tea and cookies, after filling our bellies with noodles, I told her simply that I was trans.

"Oh, Janet," Keiko said. "Thank you for telling me, but you know it's none of my damn business, right?"

"I know," I said. "But I just wanted you to hear it from me, you know?"

"I respect that," she said. "And I knew there was something about you."

"What do you mean?"

"Pretty girls are never that damn nice *and* funny," she said, laughing.

Keiko was the only person I disclosed to while in college, and I believe it's the reason we remain close. My guard has always been down with her.

Our classmate Lindsey was waiting to be heard out, so I gave her the opportunity to share her thoughts.

"Graduate and get the hell *out* of here," Lindsey said. "Why would you want to stay here any longer?"

"OK, but I feel like I need to be better-credentialed to get a job in journalism," I said. "You can't just, like, show up and start writing."

"Who says you can't?" Lindsey challenged.

"Keever, for sure," chimed Keiko, who had a strained relationship with our professor. Keever could be problematic at times, treating Keiko like a help object.

"If I were you and I was this close to graduating," Lindsey said, "I would go to New York City and get a master's there."

"*Thaaaat's* brilliant," Keiko said, shifting her head back and forth between us.

"Don't double-major," Lindsey said triumphantly. "Apply to grad school."

Getting a master's degree was something I had heard about from academics and intellectuals, book-smart, well-read, first-with-their-hands-up kinds of students. I did not see my pop-culture-obsessed self in *that* world. Of course, Lindsey, who was worldly and came from economic privilege in the Bay Area, knew all about master's degrees and grad schools. These concepts were in her orbit; they felt so far outside of mine. As a first-generation college student, I had applied to one college and did that without help from my family. Getting a bachelor's degree was as foreign an experience to my family as eating mixed greens with every meal. I came from sticky-white-rice-and-pork-eating people who had never had any words of wisdom or firsthand experience to pass on to me as I navigated my way through unknown terrain. There were no familial networks for me to tap into, no educational trust to rely on, no tangible examples of success to look to. I was too afraid to seek help because I was too afraid of being pitied.

I was a black and Native Hawaiian trans girl from a low-income, single-parent household who was about to have a damn college degree. I had already overachieved in many people's minds. *I'm good*, I thought, but people have a tendency to come into your life for many reasons, and Lindsey's was to show me the way she knew the world. She was like those traffic controllers in the middle of an intersection who yell at you, "Come on, what are you waiting for? Go!"

I went home that night and researched master's programs in journalism. I looked across the mainland, from the University of Southern California and Northwestern to Columbia and New York University, but I knew that New York was my only option. It was where I wanted to be. Troy was planning to relocate in the new year to the ship's new port in Bremerton, Washington. Before his unexpected move, we had agreed that I would graduate and move to San Diego to find a job at a local publication. Bremerton didn't appeal to me, but I didn't express my reluctance and didn't tell him I was applying to graduate school.

There was no guarantee that I would get in, anyway. I suffered from imposter's syndrome, not truly believing I was as smart as my grades, not as shiny as the awards I was given for my writing for *Ka Leo*. I was always on the verge of being found out as a fraud, a liar, a scammer. I brought all my self-doubt to Jay Hartwell, the faculty adviser at my school paper, who did the difficult work of convincing me that I was good enough. He made me internalize and appreciate the work I had put in at the school paper.

"You're more than qualified," he told me one afternoon in November in his office, a tiny space outside the newsroom shaded by the generous dome of a monkeypod tree. "I'll write a recommendation letter for you and can help you get a few solid clips published that you can include in your application package. A lot of it will rely on your personal statement."

He stressed the importance of actually bringing myself *fully* to my personal statement. He told me that my voice, my perspective, and my experiences were valuable, especially as a young woman of color from Hawaii. He viewed my background as a strength rather than a deficit. It sounded great and all, but I was reluctant to center my struggle in my application. I had been here before. I could only afford tuition because I did well in high school aided by my marginalized experience which made well-off liberals *feel* and fund my college years. This time, I yearned to be accepted on merit, on my work. I didn't want to be a charity case, someone who was let in because she had a compelling story. I didn't want to be someone who was brought in at the service of diversity alone, seen merely as a token.

"I want to get in because I'm a good writer," I argued.

"And that shows in your clips," Jay said. "But your personal statement is about filling in what they can't see on paper."

As I made my way out of his office, he called after me.

"Remember, good writers always pull from their lives," he said. "Use yours to tell a compelling story."

I went home that night and drafted my first piece of personal writing. It was a statement that talked about my multiracial family, about being the middle of five children of a mother who'd had her first baby at seventeen and a father who had struggled with drug dependency. I wrote about growing up in low-income Kalihi, where my two older sisters had become teen mothers. I wrote about both my grandmothers, who held their families together, about the scholarship from my alma mater, Farrington High, which invested in me before anyone else did. That investment allowed me to focus on a future where I saw myself working as a magazine staff writer and telling stories about culture. The only thing I kept to myself was my trans-ness. It wasn't something I felt I could use to my benefit, so I omitted that facet of myself from the narrative I crafted for acceptance.

With the personal statement behind me, I mailed my packet, took the Graduate Record Examination (GRE), and waited with crossed fingers. Four months later, I was packing my bags to spend the weekend at Aunty Lisa's house in Mililani when Mom came in with the mail.

"You have a letter from NYU," she said, handing me the envelope.

It was a slender beige envelope that seemed to hold only two sheets of paper. I was discouraged by the paltry package, but said a prayer anyway. I only prayed when I felt that the acknowledgment of a being higher than myself would tip the scales in my favor. I ripped the seal, and my eyes welled at the first line: "I am very delighted . . ."

"I got in!" I yelled, squeezing my mother tight. This pulled Chad and Jeff into the living room, where they wrapped me in their arms. *I made it*, I thought to myself. *I did it.*

"I'm so proud of you, my daughter," Mom said, as she walked with me downstairs to where Aunty Lisa was waiting in her car.

"Wow! You freaka!" my aunt said. "We have to celebrate!"

Aunty Lisa, a mother of three boys who worked as a police officer, took me to Chili's near her house, where we toasted over margaritas and Southwestern egg rolls. We spent that weekend catching up on recordings of *Oprah*. Troy called from work in Bremerton. He was on duty for the weekend, and I had been practicing how I'd tell him the news that I would be going to New York in the fall.

"I have something to share with you," I said. "I didn't want to tell you until it was a sure thing, but I got into graduate school."

I delivered the news in as neutral a tone as I could, knowing that he could be slighted by the fact that instead of going to Washington with him upon graduation, I would be in Manhattan.

"That's great, Janet," he said. "Why didn't you tell me sooner?"

"I just found out on Friday," I said.

"No, why didn't you tell me you were applying?"

"Because I didn't know if I'd get in, so I didn't want to cause any concern."

"I see. Did you apply to any schools in California?"

"No, just NYU."

He was silent on the other end, divided by an ocean and my ambition. He admired that I had my own life outside of being his wife. But by choosing a partner who was not tethered by marriage like the military wives who were steadfast in their commitment to their soldiers, he also brought himself pain.

"I'm happy for you, baby," he said.

I could tell he wanted to say more. I could tell people were around him. I could tell that this would not be the end of our conversation. I received an email a few hours later with the subject line, *You have to go*. He expressed how proud he was of me but said that his first thought was *Why am I not enough?* He wrote that the only option was for me to go. *You will resent me if you don't go, and I can't live with that*. He ended the email by saying, *I want to make this work. I love you.*

I cried reading that email but was left a bit bitter. Why did he think that I would possibly not go? I tried my best to scrape this unpleasant taste from my tongue, not wanting to acknowledge the beginning of our end. We had gone on too long relying on each other but not sharing a life. It was why I had applied to grad school without telling him. I made decisions every day that did not include him, decisions that pulled me farther and farther away from us. Nevertheless, we were married, legally bound to each other, and as my husband, he expected to be considered and factored in. He had married me. He had chosen me. He had supported me. What else did he need to do to prove that he was committed to me, that he was worth the same sacrifices from me that he made?

Troy knew what he wanted: a wife, a home, children of his own. He had stopped searching, but I was still on my quest. He was not my end, but he knew he was worthy of being someone's destination. The fact that I did not journey toward him brought him more pain than he allowed me to see, or maybe I was too selfish, too young, too narcissistic to recognize his pain.

He flew to Hawaii in May for my college graduation. I wore a green cap and gown and was surrounded by loved ones. It was a monumental moment for my family, who recognized that I was the first to break that barrier. Now that I had done it, my young nieces could see that someone in their family, someone they knew and loved, had been there and succeeded. Troy and I flew back to Washington together after that weekend. We stayed at the two-bedroom house he was renting with two other sailors. We made all the moves of a couple: watching movies, eating out, making love.

After one of our times in bed, I was naked and searching for my phone in his bedroom. I finally spotted it at the bottom of his headboard. When I reached across the carpeted floor, I was taken aback by the sight of some condoms under his bed. We had never used condoms, so I knew this meant that he had entered other bodies. When I stood, I held the condoms between my fingers as if I were holding another woman's soiled panties.

"Are you fucking other women?" I asked.

"What are you talking about?"

"Are you fucking other women?" I screamed. "Yes or no?"

"Stop being paranoid. Those are not mine."

"So someone else is hiding condoms under *your* fucking bed?"

"I guess," he said smugly.

I threw the condoms at his bare chest and slapped him across his face. My palm left a red mark on his cheek. This was what happened when you were dumb enough to let someone in, so close that they were able to hurt you. He turned and thrust his body onto me, pinning me by my wrists before jumping off the bed and escaping to the bathroom. I heard the water running and felt safe enough to cry, knowing he was in the shower.

He came back a few minutes later with a towel around his waist. His eyes matched mine—red, swollen, and weary.

"I don't think I can do this anymore," he said.

Troy usually didn't express any negativity directly when it came to us. He never wavered. Doubt did not fit his idea of what made a good man, what he thought himself to be.

"I'm in bumfuck Bremerton with this fucking ship," he said. "There is nothing here for me. *Nothing.*"

"Do you think this excuses you? That fucking other women is OK because *you have nothing?*"

"No, but you are not here," he said. "And you are not going to be here. Like why the fuck am I trying so hard?"

"Because we love each other, Troy. We try because we love each other."

"I don't think trying is enough," he said. "We are supposed to *be* together. We've been apart for longer than we were actually living together."

"That's not fair. Your job keeps us apart."

He had said all he needed to say and chose silence. He was retreating again.

"Troy? We got married!" I cried.

Married felt like a monstropolous thing, something all-encompassing that bound us in ways that felt irreversible. The thought of divorce intimidated me equally. It made me feel like a failure.

"We got married, and now you don't know if you can do this?" I pleaded. "What kind of shit is that? You're telling me that you can't do this, as if I'm a newsletter you're opting out of?"

"I just said I'm tired, Janet," he said.

I rolled my eyes at him and refused to let another tear drop. I was only a few weeks away from leaving for New York. I had planned to arrive as a young married grad student. I had planned it all out in my head. New York would be my education, and we'd figure out where to be afterward. I advocated that he could transfer to the East Coast to be near me and his family and we could commute. He had always wanted to work at the Pentagon, anyway.

I had convinced myself that we could make this work. I just needed to experience New York, get it out of my system. But Troy was not budging. He did not say he didn't want to be together; he said, "I don't think I can do this anymore."

I returned home to Hawaii unresolved and unsettled. I vacillated between *I am all that! Shit, I'm going to be a New Yorker!* and *He's the only man who will ever love me, the only one I can trust.* This monologue haunted me, circling me from despair to anger and rage, and if it weren't for my family, I would not have made it through.

The night before I left, they threw a bon voyage karaoke party for me across the street from Club Nu, where none of them knew I had worked just a year and a half before. They rented a large private room that they decorated with streamers and a customized banner: *We Will Miss You, Janet!* They got my favorite dim sum and *manapua* from Libby's and a Chantilly cake from Dee Lite Bakery that read, in red script, *Good Luck at NYU.*

Mom, Chad, Jeff, my sisters Cori-Ann and Cheraine and their kids, Aunty Lisa with her husband and her three boys, Aunty Shane with her husband and her six kids, and Grandma made it out to bid me farewell. I finally felt I was leaving the nest—the one I had with my family and the one I had with Troy. I was off into the world on my own. No one to fall back on. No one to call for financial support. I was another young dreamer leaving the comfort of home to embark on becoming who I was supposed to be.

That night was jubilant. My family showed up for me by singing off-key, eating and drinking, and cackling the only way we knew how. It was the way Papa and Grandma encouraged us to be: together in aloha. My aunts and I even had a sleepover at Aunty Lisa's place. I said good-bye to my mom that night, and we cried. Grandma told me to "be good and safe." She slipped me a card from her and Papa with a hundred dollars in it. Aunty Kanoe and Aunty Renee came with cards from my uncles. Everyone said their good-byes.

I was loved, I realized. They had so little but gave so much. Just as I had no blueprint for the things I reached for personally and professionally, my family did not have a blueprint for raising a trans child. Nevertheless, everyone was on board. They accepted and loved me for who I was, for all I wanted to be. They were consistent with their support as I embarked further on a journey that was unknown and unfamiliar to all of us. No one in my family had left Hawaii or gone to college or achieved as much as I had, but they were proud of me. I felt assured that I left my family by choice. My journey was not an escape from them in order to find myself. I was leaving the nest—finally—to discover more of myself.

PART
TWO

PART
TWO

NINE

THE FIRST DEPICTION OF NEW YORK CITY that left an indelible mark on me was the opening of *Breakfast at Tiffany's*. Holly Golightly emerges from a yellow taxi alone at dawn onto a Fifth Avenue that is emptied. The sleepy, hushed city block belongs to her. She prepares breakfast for her modern-girl self by unpacking her coffee and croissant from a white paper bag outside the iconic Tiffany & Company store. Holly finds solace in the window display after a long night out. She also takes in her own reflection—the outsider looking in.

Like the Tiffany's window, Holly was luxuriously set-dressed: the flamboyant string of pearls and impeccably highlighted bouffant, the gown, oversized sunglasses, and long gloves. She looked like New York—classic, chic, and all clean lines. She used her aesthetic to attract—and distract—gentlemen callers, men with expense accounts who didn't blink twice when she requested fifty dollars for the powder room and another fifty for cab fare. She was a hustler who promised a good time and kept the "mean reds" at bay by never allowing the men she entertained to dig deeper than the display she presented.

I was empowered by the image of the solitary single girl in the big city who had fled her small town, her family, and her husband and had shed her past and her previous selves to create herself anew. More than fifty years after Holly had taken that fateful stroll on Fifth Avenue, I landed in New York City—also alone—on a sweltering summer day in early August 2005.

I stood at the bottom of the staircase in my East Village apartment building with two heavy suitcases. My blue maxi dress's flimsy fabric stuck to my body and betrayed me by failing to conceal the sweat under my breasts. Its hem swept the black and white tile floor as I hyped myself up for the task at hand: carrying one hundred pounds of luggage up five flights. I grabbed the hem and held the slinky jersey between my front teeth. I bent down, lifted my first bag, and placed it on top of my head. I held it steady with both hands as I climbed the stairs. Once I reached the top, I left the bag outside the cracked front door, only to return to the lobby to retrieve the second one.

When I finally crossed the threshold of my apartment, I struggled to catch my breath. I rolled my luggage through a long, dark hallway with exposed brick walls and cherry hardwood floors that were uneven and slanted, creaking beneath me. The apartment was filled with unfamiliar voices strung together by random threads of conversation. *Where should we put it? This belongs in the kitchen. I can't find the box of books. Do you want this in your room? Just leave it there for now.* I was intimidated and taken aback by the assembled party in the small but bright living-room space. Three brown people were sitting hip-to-hip on a red tufted couch, rummaging through boxes. Two gray-haired white people were unwrapping flatware and glasses from newspapers at the thin kitchen bar. My roommates, Safa and Hazel, were standing with their backs toward me, holding a charcoal sketch of a woman's naked silhouette. They were consulting about where to hang the drawing.

No one had taken notice of me or heard the door open, so I cleared my throat to announce myself. Safa, in a white tank and black leggings that showed off her enviable round behind, walked toward me with open arms. She squealed as if she were greeting a childhood friend.

"Oh! My! God! You're here!" she said, enveloping me in her arms. "You guys . . . *This*! Is! Janet!"

Hazel turned toward me slowly and extended her hand, as if I were a job applicant she was meeting for an interview.

"A pleasure," Hazel said. She wore running shorts, a sports bra, and a Boston Red Sox baseball cap out of which spilled a blond ponytail.

I had met Safa and Hazel on an online message board for NYU students seeking off-campus housing. Safa's posting sought two women to share a converted three-bedroom apartment near campus that she had already secured with the help of a broker and her ophthalmologist father. *Women only, please! I want to live with considerate ladies who value cleanliness, a quiet conducive study environment, and TV veg sessions on the couch—I'll pop the popcorn :-).* Safa included a photo of herself that showed her wide, sweet smile, untamed curls, and a vaguely ethnic look that gave me a sense of belonging. I would later learn she was Egyptian.

Hazel and I were swiftly chosen, and because Hazel—a public-policy student from Cambridge, Massachusetts—was selected first, she got dibs on room choice. She chose a bedroom the same size as mine—five feet by seven feet—but whereas my room had only one window, hers had two large ones that flooded her space with direct sunlight from Avenue B. The view from her room was full of passersby and shirtless *papis* who slung their T-shirts over tan, tattooed shoulders. They never seemed to be in a rush, lounging in lawn chairs, blasting reggaeton, drinking from cans wrapped with brown paper bags, and watching theirs or someone else's kids scream as they ran through the spraying fire hydrant. They were the same guys who never failed to greet you with a *God bless you, Mami* as you passed. Despite their problematic monologues of lust, they made me feel like Jennifer Lopez in the "I'm Gonna Be Alright" music video, the one where she's playing stickball in booty shorts.

Safa and Hazel seemed like nice enough girls as they introduced me to the people settling them in: Safa's father, her younger brother and sister, Hazel's parents, and her best friend who lived in nearby Murray Hill. I shook hands with everyone, and then Hazel's father helped me pull my luggage into my bedroom. It was empty and dim, despite the sun being high in the sky that afternoon. My lone window faced the center of our six-floor tenement building, overlooking an airshaft that served as a makeshift junkyard, littered with discarded ovens, refrigerators, and other rusted appliances.

This was my first haven in New York City.

Standing in that bare space, I was struck by how big a deal it was to leave home and find your own place and how some people had others with resources to help them set up. My mother couldn't afford to travel from Honolulu with me. Plane tickets were too expensive, and she couldn't leave my brothers alone. Plus, the time off work would be a burden for her as a single working mother. I was built to rely on myself and didn't know how to ask for help or recognize that I *could* ask for help. Because of this, I had never felt so alone as I did that first night in New York, confronted by the unequivocal fact that all I had was myself—a feeling that had become all too familiar.

SOMETIMES WE FIND OURSELVES back where we were, struggling to stitch together seemingly disparate parts of our selves and our narratives, wondering how we ended up here—*again*. I was unsure whether I could escape my own patterns. One of my favorite lines in *Breakfast at Tiffany's* was "No matter where you run, you just end up running into yourself." Was I simply circling myself? It brought me back to that muggy airport terminal in Bangkok in December 2001. I was eighteen, with a small carry-on roller bag, waiting for a pair of strangers to take me to a clinic. I had sacrificed so much to take that trip and seek reconciliation with myself, by myself. I was just as afraid and just as hopeful in New York as I had been in Bangkok.

I felt overwhelmed those first days in New York, and it was easier to blame it on my long list of uncompleted tasks and the stress typically associated with moving. I didn't have the capacity then to face myself and my loneliness, to feel weary and pity myself for things I did not have. Resentment simmered in that moment toward my parents, toward my circumstance, toward my upbringing, toward Troy. But I could not afford to sit still and reflect and wallow, so I postponed my pity party. I busied myself by *doing*.

I arranged to look at a bed and a desk on Craigslist from a woman who lived a few blocks away from me on 3rd Street and Avenue D. She said she wanted $200 for the bed and $100 for the desk, but I was on a budget. I negotiated $175 for both, with cash in hand and a promise to get both items out of her apartment in the next hour. She thought it over for a beat and likely realized that she was selling a *used* mattress—a bed she had slept, lounged, and swapped fluids on—and my offer would be as good as it got. Plus, no one wanted to invite strangers into their home to inspect their belongings. She nodded, and I handed her a hundred-dollar bill as a deposit, then left with the metal bed frame in my arms.

During my two-block walk, I passed the FDNY Engine 28/ Ladder 11 fire station on 2nd Street. Its doors were open, displaying a shiny red fire truck, only made more impressive by two men—a redhead and a blond—slouched on its silver bumper. They sat with wide-legged postures, leisurely taking in the pedestrian traffic. They were unaware that they were the main attraction, with their freckled, sculpted legs in charcoal shorts and their biceps bulging from size-too-small FDNY tees. I tried my best to contain my thirst as I maintained my load, but they were the kind of men who were anxious to be called to serve.

"Need a hand, miss?" the blond fireman asked.

"Uhhhh," I said, struggling to gather my words. "Sure."

"Where you going with this?" the redhead asked.

"Home," I said.

"Where is home?" The redhead laughed as he joined me on the curb.

"Oh, down the block," I said.

"I got it," they said in unison, as they took the three pieces of metal from my arms.

"Thank you so much," I said.

"No problem." The redhead smiled. "That's what neighbors are for. Am I right?"

"Well, I have some more stuff that I need help with," I said, and I explained that I had a mattress, a box spring, and a desk that needed to be carried from an apartment on Avenue D to my apartment near Avenue B. They both beamed, elated to be of service.

The two firefighters carried my furniture down two avenue blocks and up five stories without complaint. They were drenched by the time they dropped off the last of my things at our apartment door, where my roommates and I shared our first laugh. How odd it was to be a damsel in distress rescued by two handsome firemen in supposedly unfriendly, tough-as-nails New York City. It was the perfect welcome.

I placed my full-size bed near the window and my desk parallel to the bed along the adjacent wall. I bought towels, toiletries, and a dresser from Kmart at Astor Place. I sat in the middle of my room, assembling my dresser with an Allen wrench and Kelly Clarkson's "Breakaway" blasting into my headphones. I listened to that soaring ballad on repeat in those early days. It was a salve, making me feel at ease about being alone and leaving and finding my place. It helped me believe in the wonder and promise of this city. Right around the corner stood a new friendship, some possibility, maybe even romance.

I kept my walls bare, the only decor being framed photos of my family that I placed on my dresser and desk. Grandma Pearl and my mother, siblings, aunts, and nieces were smiling all around me. On my windowsill, which served as my bedside table, I kept a silly shirt-less photo of Troy wearing my silk polka-dot head scarf across his forehead like Axl Rose.

We existed in a gray area—bound together legally yet untethered. Still, I wasn't ready to pack him up. He had become family, and he belonged here. Nevertheless, though I created a space for him in my room, I dodged his calls. I wasn't ready to talk, didn't want to engage, because I did not want to go back. I wanted to move forward. I told myself that I no longer needed him.

I was twenty-two and yearned to be carefree, without baggage (save for what I had brought up the stairs), without a backstory. I wanted to find my story here. I was single, young, and hot in the greatest city on earth. Literally hot. Having grown up in Hawaii, I was used to humidity, but this city was different. The heat was unforgiving and made my thighs slick. They rubbed together to the point where I soon developed an unbecoming case of red heat rash that my high-waist denim cutoffs couldn't hide.

All the same, I walked all over downtown, from the Lower East Side and Chinatown to SoHo, where I dropped $120 on flat red leather booties at a vintage store on Spring Street. It was one of those *I got to have it!* purchases that are fueled by personal desire and a catalog of skinny fashion-blogger images. The impulse purchase cut into the budget that would have allowed me to buy the air conditioner from P. C. Richard's that my room so needed. I justified the booties by telling myself that I hadn't grown up with AC, so why start now? The compromise made the fact that I did not have a financial safety net all too real. I would not survive in the city if I did not find a part-time job.

I had been approved for nearly fifty thousand dollars in federal and private student loans to cover tuition, books, and living expenses in America's most expensive city. It would take at least six weeks before my student-loan reimbursement check arrived for the fall semester. Picking up my Lucite heels and sheepskin rug was not an option, so I applied to boutiques in SoHo. Within a week, I landed at an over-priced denim and T-shirt shop near Wooster Street. It had air conditioning, a fifty-percent employee discount, and pay of twenty dollars an hour. I worked thirty hours a week that August, folding clothes, accessorizing and layering mannequins, and dressing women for their nights out.

The shop introduced me to my first friend in New York, a fashion designer from Ohio named Nary, who tied his straight shoulder-length black hair into a half ponytail. His forehead was adorned with a folded black bandanna, giving him a hipster street look that initially made me write him off as a wannabe gangsta. He befriended me during our first shift together by treating me to a slice of pepperoni pizza on our thirty-minute lunch break. We ate and chatted easily on a bench at Vesuvio Playground on Thompson Street.

Nary had a soft-spoken lisp that was deliberate and slow. He was never in a rush. He carried himself gently, even vulnerably. He made me *feel* for him instantly. He never solicited pity, but there was something about the way he held his eyes—a direct connection on the verge of tears—that made me feel responsible to him, even on that first lunch date.

Nary had first moved to the city in 2003 with the single goal of making it to New York Fashion Week. A self-taught and self-funded designer, he had poured all he had into showing his first collection, only to be met with a smattering of press but no orders and no means of sustaining himself or his business. He had reached his goal of making it to Fashion Week but found himself broke. He stayed afloat with the help of friends who let him crash on their sofas, before succumbing to the contradiction that New York summons artists but is too expensive for them to call it their own. Like Sylvia Plath in *The Bell Jar*, he dreamed of "steering New York like [his] own private car," but the city no longer belonged to the struggling artist. It belonged to Wall Street bros, the young guys with expense accounts and six-figure salaries who overspent on rent and crowded every club in the Meatpacking District. They let us know by the depth of their Brooks Brothers pockets that the city was theirs. They were the same men I'd soon sit across from during dinner dates at some of the hardest-to-get-into restaurants, from Babbo and the Spotted Pig to Spice Market.

As a student and a young professional, I sustained myself by dining on the dimes of insufferably boring, entitled financial-district dudes in poorly fitting suits.

"The rent is too damn high," New York politician Jimmy McMillan said, a simple statement that resonated with New Yorkers who had no financial safety net. The high cost of city living pushed Nary out and away from his dreams. Disappointed but never broken, he had moved back into his grandparents' home in Columbus and plotted his return. He worked at a fabric store, used his employee discount to get the materials needed for his next ready-to-wear collection, and returned to New York a year later. He got a job at the very boutique where we had crossed paths.

Nary was street-smart, and even though he was from Ohio and not Hawaii, he had come from the kind of world I had come from, the kind where your people love you but have nothing but love to offer. If there were visions we wanted to pursue, we knew that we would have to chase after them on our own. This common pursuit cemented our friendship. Nary taught me how to navigate the city and fight hunger with very little money—pho and dim sum spots in Chinatown, bottomless mimosa brunches, two-for-one taco stands, art galleries with endless pours. He networked his way onto every downtown party promoter's list, and I became one of the stylish girls he adorned himself with. The bevy of feminine beauty gave him all-you-can-drink access.

I still have the selfies from the first party we attended together at the Maritime Hotel. It was a release party for a single-issue fashion zine. The party venue was adorned with gold and silver balloons, filled-to-the-rim champagne flutes, and barefoot dancers wearing nothing but rose-gold body paint. I remember dancing lustfully with the Dominican model Omahyra, badgering columnist Michael Musto until he agreed to read my clips, and busting the strap on the dress I had borrowed from the boutique. It was one of those parties that ended with me squeezing Nary around his neck and screaming into his ear, "I love you so much!" This would become our signal that it was time for me to get home before the world began to spin and the night's house vodka ended up splattered on the cement.

I walked to my apartment that night on a high. It was one A.M., and I didn't want to break the crisp twenty-dollar bill in my clutch on cab fare. It took me thirty minutes to walk crosstown in heels, sobering me up just in time to set my stiletto-clad feet on Avenue A. The sight of rats scurrying in the dark around Tompkins Square Park, the young and nodding heroin addicts with their handwritten signs calling for comfort, the sweet smell of Ray's greasy beignets, and Jim Power's mosaic light poles began to signal home.

No one knew me as well as those East Village streets back then. They saw me for what I was: young, alone, afraid, anxious, excited, lusty, heartbroken, eager, weary, yearning, seeking. They were my witness, watching me as I set my Trader Joe's bags on the ground to catch my breath, as I wiped my mouth with the back of my hand after sloppily kissing some boy on St. Mark's Place, as I wondered about whether I was good enough, pretty enough, smart enough, as I psyched myself up for a first date, an internship interview, and the first day of school. Perhaps no one would ever know me quite as well.

"I FEEL MOST COLORED when I am thrown against a sharp white background," Zora Neale Hurston wrote in her 1928 essay "How It Feels to Be Colored Me," where she described her "sea change" from "everybody's Zora" in the all-black town of Eatonville, Florida, to the "little colored girl" at age thirteen when she was sent to school with white people in Jacksonville. She spoke about her time at Barnard College, where, she wrote, "I feel my race. Among the thousand white persons, I am a dark rock surged upon, overswept by a creamy sea. I am surged upon and overswept, but through it all, I remain myself. When covered by the waters, I am; and the ebb but reveals me again."

The themes of Hurston's essay speak to my experience at New York University and all of downtown Manhattan, where whiteness dominated. I was one of five black people in my graduate program, and we were all women. We, the five black girls, maintained just enough distance to feel cradled but not too close as to make our peers feel as if we were huddling and conspiring. We were close enough to give one another the *I see you, black girl* nod. We were close enough to throw one another a swift side-eye as affirmation of someone's showing their ass. We were close enough to offer praise or affirmation when the rest of the room fell silent. We showed up for one another in ways that enabled us to survive graduate school, where it often felt as if we were not there to get an education but to provide our peers a diverse learning experience with our mere presence.

Still, I left NYU without a friendship in tow. I was very much that one girl—some may call her the villainous bitch, I call her an inspiration—seen on every season of *America's Next Top Model*. She's the contestant who screams during her confessional, *I did not come here to make friends. I came here to be America's Next Top Model.*

We were a generation of journalism students who grew up and worshipped print—newspapers, books, and magazines—but gathered most of our news online, from blogs, news websites, and social media. We were paying tens of thousands of dollars to gain experience, training, and credentials that would make us marketable in a rapidly shifting media landscape. As it had been at the University of Hawaii, the buzzword was still *new media*, but its meaning had gone beyond the bland *anything beyond traditional print and television* to the paranoid *print is being threatened by young people on the Internet, and we do not know what to do, so we will reluctantly embrace digital.*

Our professors were evangelists for print, so they forced us to subscribe to the *New York Times*, because, as journalists, they claimed, we needed to invest in organizations that were paying journalists in the age of new media. Digital journalism seemed to be met with reluctance and skepticism in the program, with the exception of Adam

Penenberg, who had made a name for himself on Forbes.com in 1998 by unmasking the *New Republic*'s Stephen Glass as a serial fabricator. In addition to pushing us to report on our neighborhoods, Penenberg required us to create and maintain a class blog, where we wrote entries about our experiences reporting on the streets of New York. (This piece of advice from him has never left me: "Never search for stories on the ground floor. Be a tourist in your neighborhood. Always look up. You'll find stories waiting to be told on the second floor.") It acted as a reporter's notebook that trained us for the digital age. It felt like a chore at the time to submit three entries a week for the blog, but Penenberg was training us to write and file stories quickly and accurately, to editorialize our experiences as reporters, and to distinguish between what should be reserved for our articles and what material would be more suitable for a blog entry. These were tools that would come in handy when we entered the marketplace as interns, entry-level reporters, fact checkers, and editorial assistants.

I came to NYU with the singular goal of becoming a features editor for a women's magazine. I often felt out of place in our program because of my focus on fashion and popular culture. Unlike my peers, I rarely read daily papers, never watched cable news, and had no interest in politics. My news outlets consisted of the Superficial, Go Fug Yourself, Perez Hilton, *People*, *Jane*, and *Vanity Fair*. I planned to embark on a media career that would make use of all the *junk* I had gathered in my head from years of watching *TRL*, *Golden Girls*, and *Designing Women* reruns—and from award shows.

Pop culture had always offered me an escape. My aversion to hard news had a lot to do with the grim reality that seemed to permeate news. Throughout the summer and early fall, the Gwen Araujo murder trial was in the papers. Her tragic death at age seventeen in 2002, at the hands of men with whom she had been sexually involved, was one I wanted to avoid. Hers was my worst nightmare. I wanted to leave the darker, tougher aspects of my reality behind.

It irked me that my professors pushed me to go outside of what entertained me and report on issues that held much higher stakes than Team Angie versus Team Jen. My graduate program's collective push toward hard news led me to Julio, a sixty-four-year-old man who resided in a transitional living center a few blocks from my apartment on the Bowery. I had passed it many times on my way to class and noted the fenced courtyard on the east side of the building, because it resembled a prison yard. It was a block I made sure to avoid when it was dark, but by day, I was struck by the building's presence in a quickly gentrifying East Village. It was a relic of the neighborhood's darker past, and it remained among luxury hotels, chic restaurants, and expensive boutiques. One afternoon, my curiosity led me to strike up a conversation with a man who was smoking a cigarette across the street from the building. He was leaning with a casual elegance against a brick wall, as if he were on his own porch.

"Excuse me, sir," I said, on my way home from class one late afternoon. "What is that building?"

"That one?" he said, pointing at the eight-story building.

I nodded.

"It's a halfway house for men," he said nonchalantly. "I live there."

His skin looked like well-used corkboard, tan and filled with texture. He had short, dark hair that lay softly like a newborn baby's. He reminded me of my paternal grandfather, a man who sported his masculinity lightly. We always knew he was in charge, but we were never frightened. It was this quality that led me to introduce myself as a journalism student and ask if he would be interested in allowing me to write a story about him.

"No one's ever wanted to write about me," Julio said, shrugging his shoulders. "Nothing really to tell." His nonchalance, humility, and economy of language only made me want to write about him more.

"What if I treat you to a cup of coffee this week?" I offered.

"I don't drink coffee," he said.

"Tea, then?"

"I like hot chocolate." He grinned, his two front teeth missing.

A few days later, I took Julio to the Bean on 3rd Street. He sat across from me and slurped his hot chocolate like a giddy kindergartner. He had no qualms about the recorder that sat on the bistro table between us or the yellow legal pad I was taking notes on. As a student, I was taught that I needed to take myself out of the story and remain objective—as if I brought nothing but the skills of reporting, interviewing, sourcing, researching, and writing to the table. I was told not to bring a perspective or an opinion. These tenets led me to approach my initial conversations with Julio as a reporter, asking a series of sterile fact-finding questions: *How old are you? Do you have children? Where are they? Did you raise them? Why were you so absent?* Then maybe a more probing one: *When did you commit your first crime?* My questions got me nowhere with Julio. He'd irritatingly avoid my questions by telling me stories that seemed irrelevant or by asking me questions about my own life. I began to treat my time with him as work and saw our conversations as a means to an end, the end being my class final, an eight-thousand-to-ten-thousand-word piece about my New York neighborhood.

It wasn't until I stopped asking questions and began actually listening that he opened up and gave testimony. Bearing witness, rather than seeking answers, filled me. He told me about his early childhood in the Dominican Republic, about moving to the Bronx when he was thirteen, about the prevalence and normalcy of the drug trade in the public housing complex in which he had grown up. In high school, Julio thought he'd be a baseball player, but he wasn't skilled enough to go from JV to varsity. Without baseball, he found school boring, a place where he didn't excel in class or with girls, so he dropped out. The only options for a high school dropout were gangs and the drug trade.

"I wasn't tough enough for that," he said.

Instead of selling drugs, Julio did them. Soon he found himself chasing a high and committing small crimes to support his addiction. Pickpocketing subway riders and pawning his mother's silver emboldened him to hold up a bodega at knifepoint. He did twenty years for attempted armed robbery and possession of drugs.

"I missed everything," he said. "My daughter won't even talk to me. You remind me of her a little bit. The eyes and the coloring."

My conversations with Julio throughout the fall raised my consciousness about systemic oppression. Our culture and policies did not look at addiction as a health issue; instead, we criminalized poor folk and people of color struggling with drug dependency. Julio's drug use led him to commit crimes that slapped him with a felony conviction, which stripped him of his right to vote and made him less than desirable in the job market.

Writing about Julio not only helped me connect dots between him and our social, economic, and criminal justice systems, but it also connected dots between Julio and me. I never saw those connections when we were chatting in the coffee shop; I only noticed how familiar his story felt when I transcribed our conversations alone in my bedroom.

I had parents who struggled with poverty, a lack of opportunity, and substance abuse. I hadn't come to New York and invested all I had, and didn't have, only to be reminded of trauma and injustice and home. I resisted creating work that reflected my experience. I had fought so hard to survive, persevere, and ultimately escape my past. I turned the lens out so I didn't have to deal with what was within.

It was not lost on me that I was living a block away from legendary trans activists Marsha P. Johnson's and Sylvia Rivera's first location for STAR (Street Transvestite Action Revolutionaries) House. I spent most of my time in the same neighborhood as the Stonewall Inn, the site of the 1969 riots that ignited the modern LGBTQ rights movement. I went to school only blocks away from the West Side Highway, where generations of trans, gender-nonconforming, and queer folk sought refuge and community.

Pretending felt safest. I believed it was the only way I could make it. So I stripped myself of backstory and connection and flattened myself, distilled myself, made myself smaller and easier to contain and digest. I pretended that color, class, gender, and all the intersections of my identity and experience that *othered* me did not exist. And the funny thing was that my classmates, roommates, and neighbors were pleased to pretend, too. It made it easier on all of us to believe a postracial, postfeminist, postoppression fantasy, especially in a well-intentioned liberal New York City.

Playing pretend was why I had always loved the movies, entertainment, and all things Hollywood. It was an industry that sold fantasy and provided escape, giving kids like me a reprieve from harsh realities. Though I earned an A for my feature on Julio, I knew I would not be *going there* for a living. I'd leave politics and "hard news" to my peers, who were all too eager to set their lenses and pens on the marginalized. Reporting across difference enabled them to feel purposeful and use their race and class privilege for the greater good. They could be do-gooders. I was committed more than ever to culture.

TEN

I SPENT MOST OF MY TIME that first semester alone in my room listening to Kanye West's *The College Dropout* and *Late Registration* and leaning against my windowpane, peering at my neighbors. This pastime became so routine that I gave some of them names and narratives, as if they were dolls in my own Manhattan playhouse. My favorite neighbor to watch was a forty-plus Latina I called Esmeralda. I had a clear view of her oval-shaped face and long, slender torso through a narrow kitchen window. She was either facing me at her sink or with her back toward me using her stovetop. She draped a red quilt over her shoulders as if it were a shawl, even on warm days. She lived alone, never had company, and moved about her apartment as if she were floating. She possessed the beauty of someone of an indeterminate age—she could have been forty-three, fifty-eight, or sixty-seven. Initially, I thought she was a painter, because she twisted her dark brown hair into a slick, unfussy updo held with a long, thin paintbrush. But the way she took her time, with a delicate, calculated grace—whether she was pouring boiling water from her kettle or scrubbing skillets—

convinced me that she had to be a dancer or a chorus girl. Maybe she was an artist's muse.

If one of my neighbors had watched me in my own kitchen, it wouldn't have been nearly as intriguing. I was limited when it came to cooking, because my single working mother raised us on Hamburger Helper, frozen dinners, and packaged taco mixes. Now I subsisted on boiled eggs and toast, cans of tuna on King's Hawaiian rolls, baked chicken with instant bags of white rice, Trader Joe's frozen burritos, and ramen with a cracked egg, wilted mixed greens, and sriracha. Meanwhile, my roommate Hazel had left the nest as a full-fledged adult who could nourish herself. She spent her Sundays planning meals at the Union Square farmers market and Whole Foods. Our narrow breakfast bar would be stacked with plastic containers filled to the rim with freshly prepared, perfectly portioned lunches and dinners—quinoa and bean salads, hearty vegetable soups, brussels sprouts drenched in bacon grease—that would take up her assigned row in the refrigerator.

Our apartment smelled like lavender, shea butter, and microwave popcorn—Safa's favorite snack. She could most often be found on the couch, with her short, thick legs extended to the coffee table. Her favorite shows were *American Idol* and Anthony Bourdain's travel show, *No Reservations*. For Hazel and me, the living room was a space we passed on our way to the bathroom and the kitchen. But for Safa, who was eager to connect, the living room was a common space, where she tried her hardest to lure us out of our caves.

I chose my own company in my own room because I was laser-focused on school and protective of the clear boundaries I had set. I didn't want to get too personal, too friendly, and too messy. Beyond an initial dinner at Il Bagatto, the restaurant on the ground floor of our building, I didn't socialize with my roommates. Our daily conversations were limited to the exchange of a few cordial words about the weather, class and study loads, and weekend plans. It also didn't help that Hazel and I had made it clear that we'd prefer not to pay for cable when Safa stated that she *needed* it.

"I can't miss *American Idol*," Safa said, talking more to herself than to us. "Plus, *Grey's Anatomy* is coming back in September."

Hazel was unmoved, but I was eager for *Grey's* season two return. My budget could not handle another utility bill, so I sided with Hazel that my limit was Internet. Though it was an awkward negotiation, Safa was unfazed. Still, it created a dynamic that kept me out of the living room, away from where the cable TV Safa paid for was located.

Budgeting didn't seem like a priority for Safa. But she was kind, down-to-earth, and connected to the struggle, having grown up in Memphis and taught at public schools in nearby black communities. She was intent on returning to Tennessee to be a school administrator and influence policy. Still, she couldn't conceal her inner rich girl. She furnished our apartment, ate out at least three times a week, ordered her groceries from Fresh Direct, and treated herself to nightly deliveries of tacos, burgers, and wings and fries.

One Sunday that September, Safa ordered too many entrees from Raj Mahal on 6th Street to celebrate the season premiere of *Grey's Anatomy* (this was before it would move to its long-held Thursday-night slot). The indulgence gave her an opportunity to socialize. She knocked on our bedroom doors and offered us free meals, which would have been rude for me to decline. I ate a plate of peshwari naan, chicken biryani, and beef madras on the narrow breakfast counter, as Safa and Hazel enjoyed their food on the couch. We were all silent as we waited for the premiere to begin. When a teaser for the episode aired, we all squealed in excitement.

"Ugh, I love *Grey's*," Safa said.

"I know, me, too!" I added, sucking tomato sauce off my fingers.

"I hope Meredith dumps his married ass!" Hazel said.

Shonda Rhimes's first television series had reached all of us, from our places of becoming in Memphis, Cambridge, and Honolulu. I had fallen in love with *Grey's* on my mother's couch during the final semester of undergrad. It was a midseason replacement that spoke to me as a young woman embarking on my own career. I hated procedurals and hadn't watched a hospital show before but was hooked by the narrative of this boozy, slutty, super-flawed intern who was ambitious yet tortured by her painful childhood with her super-accomplished mother. She was the messy girl we all couldn't help but love—or passionately argue about. Sure, Patrick Dempsey's dimples and full head of hair were draws, but it was an entertaining, sudsy show that centered a woman's narrative, gave us dishy elevator hookups, and treated people of color as if they were people.

"We should watch it together!" Safa suggested.

"Can we?" I pleaded.

"Of course!" Safa said.

I washed my hands and rinsed my plate clean and squeezed in next to Safa on the couch, as *Grey's* picked up right up where it had left us. We sat in silence, not even speaking during commercials. This became our weekly routine. Someone ordered dinner, and we watched *Grey's Anatomy* together. It became appointment television. We were as obsessed with the goings-on at Seattle Grace as Cristina Yang was about slicing patients open. We sat hip-to-hip on the couch for an entire season, which had the effect of making us slowly but surely reveal ourselves to one another.

Routine and closeness had a way of creating comfort, and our apartment became a home, something far more than a place where we stored our stuff, made food, slept, and showered. *Grey's* made us grow closer, and it made me step outside the walls I had built.

"Her boobs are *so* fake!" Hazel screamed at the TV one Sunday, as Katherine Heigl walked across the screen in her bra.

"No," I said, "those are real."

"They're too big to be real," Hazel said.

"Well, as a big-breasted woman," Safa chimed in, "I agree with Janet. They're definitely real."

"You see how they slope downward instead of standing up?" I pointed at the screen. "That's how you know."

"Well, yours kind of stand up," Hazel said, as she reached across Safa and poked my right breast with her finger. As was my routine in the apartment, I wasn't wearing a bra, just a beige tank top. I never presumed they were points of fascination at home. I knew Hazel meant to strike a playful jab, but I was offended by her questioning. I was more upset with myself, though, for growing too comfortable around her.

"They do, don't they?" I said in mock fascination. "Guess I'm lucky."

"I wish mine stayed in place," Safa said, trying to release the tension. "I've always wanted to get mine lifted."

"You're perfect," Hazel said, as if Safa—the big girl in our house— were fishing for a body-positive compliment. "But are they?" she asked me. "Are they real?"

"You were poking at them because you think they're fake, right?" I said. "So why do you need an answer?"

My outrage squeezed between us on the couch. Safa began fidgeting with the kernels at the bottom of her popcorn bowl. She seemed to be searching for a way out.

"Well, it's just a question," Hazel said, unable to apologize, drop it, or fight her desire for confirmation. She felt entitled to get to the bottom of it. "You don't have to answer. I didn't mean to offend you."

"Oh, I'm not offended *at all*," I snapped.

I let the silence linger for a bit, then grew defiant.

"I had my boobs done when I was nineteen," I said. "I grew up in Hawaii. Everyone has their boobs done."

"Really?" Safa jumped in. "That's interesting, because a lot of women in my culture get nose jobs. My sister has one."

"Yeah, plastic surgery isn't a big deal back home," I said.

"That's really young," Hazel said. "Your body doesn't stop maturing until you're twenty-one. And it's so expensive."

Before she could ask me how I paid for it, I stood up from the couch and walked to the kitchen to refill my glass of wine. I knew

Hazel was digging now, and I had been too careless to realize that my plastic-surgery revelation did not align with who they knew me to be: a single girl from a working-class family in Hawaii who never joined them for dinner dates out. I could see Hazel's wheels spinning behind her furrowed brow. She was always questioning, always seeking. Her prosecutorial delivery always betrayed her well-meaning intentions. I was never that curious. I always felt people would tell me their business if they wanted to.

"I just never knew someone who had it done," Hazel said when I came back into the room.

"Well, we do now," Safa said, attempting to end the conversation.

"A lot of people have stuff done that we do not know about," I said. "People don't walk around with their medical records at the ready."

"Fair enough," Hazel said. I soon learned that when she said *fair enough*, it was her way of saying *I do not agree with you, but I'll leave it alone and sit in judgment.*

"I still want to get my boobs reduced," said Safa, who adapted to her role of peacemaker.

I left that conversation bitter and festered in the privacy of my room. We returned to *Grey's*, but Sundays at home never felt the same again. My distaste for Hazel became difficult to conceal. When I heard her voice, I'd roll my eyes. When I saw her blond ponytail poking out of the back of her Red Sox cap, I'd roll my eyes. When I smelled sautéed brussels sprouts, I'd roll my eyes. The apartment became unbearable, and I wanted to minimize my time around her.

I had quit my retail job in October as soon as my reimbursement check cleared, which enabled me to concentrate on school. Once I settled into a routine, I set my sights on securing an internship for the spring semester. I applied for listings on Ed2010.com, a social network that connected aspiring magazine editors to internship and job opportunities. The collective goal was for us all to become editors in five years—by the year 2010. I was eager to build my résumé beyond my retail experience in overpriced boutiques. I applied to about a dozen postings, with little to no response, before coming across an internship that not only offered class credit but also paid students ten dollars an hour. It was for *Playboy* magazine.

I had never read the magazine before. All I knew was the life-style projected by Hugh Hefner and the blond bombshells who had transcended their centerfold status to become pop-cultural figures— Pamela Anderson, Jenny McCarthy, and the late, great Anna Nicole Smith. I hadn't known that *Playboy* was one of the last monthly maga-zines that published fiction, that its archives included short stories from Margaret Atwood, Haruki Murakami, and Gabriel García Márquez; essays by James Baldwin and Gore Vidal; and landmark interviews such as Alex Haley's with Martin Luther King Jr. I didn't know that Truman Capote, the author of *Breakfast at Tiffany's*, spoke about his motivations for creating his iconic character in the magazine in 1968: "The main reason I wrote about Holly, outside of the fact that I liked her so much, was that she was such a symbol of all these girls who come to New York and spin in the sun for a moment like mayflies and then disappear. I wanted to rescue one girl from that anonymity and preserve her for posterity."

I wanted to be rescued from the slush pile of email applications for this rare paid internship. The career counselor in our journalism program advised us to write letters that summarized our editorial experience and highlighted our voices and perspectives. I consulted her one-on-one about possibly taking a risky move for a seemingly risqué magazine. She said, "Don't be afraid to stand out." That was all the push I needed to put myself out there—in a big way—in my cover letter, which opened with this line: "I am uniquely qualified to be *Playboy*'s next editorial intern wielding three years of editorial staff experience, three features writing awards, a forthcoming master's degree from NYU, and a 34D."

I went up to *Playboy*'s swanky office on Fifth Avenue, wearing a charcoal sheath dress I had bought for eighty-nine dollars at Zara. It was the most I had ever spent on a dress, but I justified the purchase by dubbing it my interview uniform. I was met in the lobby by a short, bearded, bald man who couldn't have been more than five years older than I was. He introduced himself as Ross and walked me over to an empty conference room with poster-size copies of *Playboy*'s most recent covers.

Ross was a proud Jersey boy who had worked his way up from intern to editorial assistant and now was assistant editor. The internship program was under his sole stewardship. He was direct, super-chill, and an evangelist for all things *Playboy*.

"Can we talk about your cover letter?" he asked.

"Sure," I said, a bit embarrassed by his forwardness.

"It was a bold move." He laughed. "I never read a cover letter like that before. I knew I had to meet you."

"All I wanted to do was get your attention," I said.

"Major props," he said. "OK, so what do you know about the magazine?"

"On the surface, it wouldn't be a magazine that I would read."

"Because of the pictorials?"

"No, because it's a men's magazine," I said.

"That makes sense."

"The photos don't bother me. I'm not a prude," I said. "What women do with their bodies is their business, and I have no qualms about pornography—"

"What we do is *not* pornography," Ross interrupted, casually stating a universal truth known only within the halls of *Playboy*. "It is a men's magazine that fulfills our readers' fantasies about beautiful women who like sex and informs them about society so they can have something smart to say."

I just nodded in silence, hoping I hadn't offended him or come off as uptight. Ross, who had no idea about my past in the sex industry, was used to defending the magazine's editorial integrity. This defense was in *Playboy*'s DNA. I didn't question the brand's sexual politics, because I didn't feel torn about working for a magazine that published photographs of women who chose to disrobe for cameras. It was their body, their image, and if they were OK with it, who was I to argue against a woman's choice? My intentions were all too selfish, anyway. I wanted to get in the door and secure my first internship with a long-established magazine. I had no feminist agenda to combat the patriarchy.

"What writers do you love?" Ross asked.

"I've been reading a lot of nonfiction lately and have fallen for Gay Talese and Joan Didion. Some longtime favorites are Toni Morrison, Jane Austen, and James Baldwin."

"What magazines do you subscribe to?"

"*Vanity Fair, Vogue,* the *New Yorker,* and *Jane.*"

"Finally, why did you apply to *Playboy*?"

"You pay and give class credit, which we both know is rare," I said. "Most important, I just want the experience, and working at *Playboy* will give me something to talk about. People are intrigued—good or bad—by the brand."

"Awesome," Ross said, and he stood up from his chair, signaling the end of our interview. We made our way through a long hallway with mockups of the next issue posted on the walls. There were interviews with former Playmates, a short story, satirical cartoons, and centerfolds.

"You get used to it pretty quickly," Ross said, as he shook my hand and handed me a stack of the most recent issues—a common parting gift for any magazine interview.

On my ride home on the F Train, I flipped through an issue with a bikini-clad Jessica Alba on its cover that boasted an interview with Kanye West, an artist who had provided a soundtrack to my own collegiate years. Just six months earlier, the rapper-producer had ditched the script during NBC's live broadcast of a benefit concert for Hurricane Katrina victims and stated that "George Bush doesn't care about black people." In the *Playboy* interview, he said that the NBC producers "didn't really listen to [his songs] 'All Falls Down' and 'Jesus Walks' and 'Crack Music.' They just heard the hooks. They didn't hear what I was saying about social issues. With my polo collars popped, they never saw me coming."

A few hours later, Ross called to offer me the internship, and I started the following week. Most of my work involved organizing the magazine archive, transcribing interviews with former Playmates for front-of-the-book vignettes, and assisting the *Playboy* Adviser Chip Rowe on research for a series he was writing about the sexual life, from conception to death, of the American male. I felt useful and respected—and not once was I asked to fetch someone's coffee or lunch.

Initially, it was jarring to see images of nude women tacked up on the walls without discretion. I never took issue with the common-place display of naked female bodies in the office, but I did wonder if these silent female forms shaped the way my male colleagues viewed my own young woman's body. Eventually, the novelty of bare breasts wore off, and I realized that we were just a bunch of journalists, working in cubicles and trying to make deadline.

There were no casting calls, no photography studios, no Bunnies. Hugh Hefner and his girlfriends—who were ubiquitous because of the popularity of the E! reality series *The Girls Next Door*—didn't stop by the New York offices (at least, not when I was there). The closest I ever got to Hef was sharing an elevator with his daughter Christie Hefner, the CEO of Playboy Enterprises, who had run her father's company for more than thirty years. It felt ironic yet appropriate that a company centering the heterosexual American male experience, desire, and gaze, and one that profited from the bare female form, was run by a woman.

I left *Playboy* with a quicker, sharper wit, the ability to make any headline into a sexual pun, and a realistic portrait of what it took to churn out a monthly magazine. My time there would remain one of the most fulfilling professional experiences I would have, and it would further affirm my desire and intent to work in magazine publishing.

I TOLD SAFA I did not want to celebrate my twenty-third birthday, but I still arrived home from school to a house filled with the scent of freshly baked cake and warm tortilla shells. I ran into the kitchen and slapped Safa on her round behind.

"*Girl*, did I *not* tell you?" I exclaimed in faux anger.

"Deal with it," she said. "It's your birthdaaaaay."

I grabbed a shell from the cookie sheet and crunched into it. "OK, tell me your plan," I said.

"It's not a plan *at all*," she said, as she stirred the ground turkey in the skillet. "I invited a few friends over. We're gonna have dinner, eat some cake, drink some wine, and maybe dance."

"What about Hazel?" I asked.

"She's got a date tonight," she said, knowing full well that I could not stand Hazel. Safa tried her best to be friends with both of us by scheduling things with one of us when the other one was committed elsewhere.

"I see you thought of everything," I said, as I reached for a strawberry. Safa smacked my hand.

"Those are for the cake," she said, pointing to a vanilla cake with whipped cream frosting. It was her specialty. "Now, stop worrying and *please* get ready."

I poured a glass of white wine, skipped into my room, and applied heavy coats of mascara, blush, and lipstick. I put on a backless black halter and a pair of low-rise Hudson jeans. By eight P.M., our dinner party arrived: my friend Nary; Safa's classmate Cecilio, whom she had met during a student exchange in Barcelona; and Safa's sister Ebe, an ophthalmology student who lived in Boston. The five of us sat down to eat tacos and take back as much red sangria and Coronas as our bellies could handle. Just as Safa was putting the last strawberry halves on the cake, the front door opened.

"Oh, my God! Please remind me *never* to get set up again," Hazel said, stomping through the hallway. "It was literally the worst night of my life."

Safa looked at me with her wide hazel eyes and mouthed, *Sorry!* I could not believe that I would have to tolerate Hazel on my birthday.

"Oh, honey! I'm sorry," Safa said to Hazel, not missing a beat. "You want something to drink?"

Hazel nodded and threw her purse on her bed, unbothered by the fact that she was interrupting a dinner party.

"What did you guys eat?" she asked.

"Tacos," Cecilio said through his Spanish accent, which always made everything sound so much more enticing.

"Have you ever sat across from someone and regretted committing to a full meal?" Hazel asked the room as she took a seat.

"Never," Nary said. "I always take girls out to coffee or drinks. Dinner is too expensive."

"I do the same thing," Cecilio said.

"You guys are so *cheap!*" Ebe protested.

"Well, I wish we only had drinks tonight!" Hazel continued. "The guy was pasty, bald, pudgy, and a bore! I'm kicking Melissa's ass when I see her."

"That's terrible," Safa said, handing her a glass of sangria.

"The worst," Ebe added, raising her glass to meet Hazel's.

I smiled in pity and stood up to walk to the bathroom to fix my face. I knew that if I did not give myself a pep talk, we would likely end up pulling out each other's hair. The tension was that thick, and I wanted to show a bit of effort, because Safa had put in so much work to ensure that this night was special for me. I could at least avoid rolling my eyes at Hazel for one night. It proved to be a difficult task, because she was not just complaining; she was performing victimhood. She wanted to be catered to, to be pitied. It was the only way she knew to be as an only child.

"Well, we were just getting ready to cut the cake," I heard Safa say as I made my way back to the living room.

"Oh, my God! I forgot it's her birthday." Hazel giggled. She was trolling me now.

"Jaaaaanet!" Safa called. She placed the cake at the center of the table and wielded her long red lighter. "Time to light your candles!"

I took a few deep breaths, walked down the hallway, and took my seat at the head of the table. The fact that Hazel was seated at the opposite end did not shake me. I concentrated on the flickering light in the room from the candles. I closed my eyes to shut out everyone around me and made my birthday wish: *I want my own apartment and a job once I graduate.* I opened my eyes, exhaled a deep, long breath that extinguished all light, and was met with applause in the darkness. Safa turned on the lights and sliced the cake.

Cecilio, ever the flirt, said, "If it were my birthday, I'd wish for you, my darling."

I giggled at his corniness, and Hazel let out an obnoxious cackle.

"That's very sweet, Cecilio," I said, reaching across the table to touch his shoulder.

"Oh, my God," Hazel said. "Get a room, already!"

I rolled my eyes at her as I stuffed my face with cake, and I committed then and there to push her in her vomit if she threw up that night.

"Can we please get a picture together before we get too drunk?" Safa asked, as we gathered our things to head to Babel, a hookah bar that played Top 40 on Avenue C.

Hazel, Safa, and I gathered close, with Safa in the center. I felt Hazel's eyes on me. It could have been the constant refills of sangria or the jealousy that stemmed from Cecilio's lusting eyes or the visibility of my body, but she refused to stay put.

"No one wants me in this photo," she said, tipsy and fishing for a compliment. "I can tell!"

"You all look so hot," Cecilio said, "like a United Colors of Benetton billboard."

Safa giggled. "We really do look good."

"OK, but I'll only take it if she puts those away," Hazel said, and she reached across Safa to slap my right breast. It stung a bit.

"What is it with you and my boobs?" I snapped. "You're fucking obsessed!"

Ebe, Nary, Cecilio, and Safa turned to me, anticipating a girl fight. Don't get me wrong. I was very close to slapping her, but I took a breath and faked a loud laugh.

"I'm kidding!" I said. "I'll turn around, then."

My exposed back faced Cecilio as I joined Safa and Hazel in a full, fake, tense smile.

"You're so hot," Cecilio said as he clicked the camera.

As soon as we got to the bar, I began taking shots I hadn't paid for. Tequila. Jack. Lemon drops. I began chanting 50 Cent's lyrics: *And you know we don't give a fuck it's not your birthday!* I drank so aggressively that my hard exterior softened, and I let Cecilio in. He had been trying to get my attention for months. I knew he was that guy in every friend group that every girl eventually makes out or sleeps with. I didn't care. He felt like a safe bet, a low-stakes hookup.

"You're a queen among mortals," he whispered in my ear as he held me close on the dance floor. "You know that already."

I laughed at him, as I always did when he talked. His delivery was as dramatic as that of a telenovela star exiting a scene.

"Shut up, Cecilio," I said, shrugging off his effort to woo me. "Let's just dance. No talking!"

"I am not kidding," he said. "You never take me serious, which is smart of you. But I am serious. You come from another planet."

He looked at me unflinchingly. The way he held my eyes sobered me up for a few brief seconds. I gained enough clarity to realize that he *saw* me. He was not searching for answers. He *knew.* I did not know what he knew, but I felt seen. It was an intense, intimate, and surprising exchange that led me to tell him, "It's time to go."

We rushed out of the club and kissed and grabbed each other as we walked to my building. It was nearly one A.M. when I turned the key to the front door of my lobby. It was quiet and still, except for our sloppy steps and kisses. I tripped on the second flight of stairs and fell. I was too drunk to be embarrassed or inhibited. The black and white tile of the stairwell seemed like a good enough location for sex. I pulled Cecilio by the arm toward me. We relished our first sliver of privacy and giggled as he climbed into me.

WHEN I GOT INTO NYU, the first person outside my family I told about my acceptance was Lela, my fashion merchandising friend from UH. As I relayed my plans to move to New York over the summer, her broad smile hardened. I was taken aback by her less-than-warm response.

"I've never told anyone this," she said with a deep wistfulness, "but I've always wanted to live in New York."

I realized that my good news had reactivated a long-dormant dream for Lela. She was happy for me but also envious that she didn't have a clear path to that dream. Lela explained that moving to New York was the only way she'd get off the retail floor at Christian Dior and move into corporate. She was tired of just selling clothes. She wanted to build a career in merchandising.

"Once I get set up, you have an open invitation to stay with me," I said. "I'm serious."

It was the kind of courtesy you extended not expecting the other person to redeem your offer. No matter how chic and sophisticated I thought Lela was, I still saw her as a local girl—and local girls *never* leave Hawaii. But as soon as I'd unpacked my suitcases, I began receiving emails from Lela full of questions. She wanted to know how my apartment search went, what the square footage was, how many roommates I had, what the rent, broker's fee, and security deposit had cost. She was doing her research and told me that she planned to move in the spring and would like to take me up on my offer of a crash pad. Knowing what I knew about her dream, I decided to oblige.

Lela arrived in New York a few weeks after my birthday in late March and stayed with me for a week as she hunted for apartments in the East Village. She met two Chinese guys online who worked in finance and signed a lease with them for a spot on 13th Street and First Avenue within her first two days. That's how fast the city moved. One day you came with nothing but your belongings, the next you owed your landlord a few thousand dollars. To celebrate Lela's Big Apple move, she and I spent a rainy Friday afternoon at the Museum of Modern Art. We were sipping lattes as we strolled through a crowded Warhol exhibit, when Lela leaned over a railing and moaned.

"Is everything OK?" I asked, concerned.

"These cramps are killer," she said, as she pressed her palm into her abdomen. "I just need a minute."

"Do you want to find a seat?"

"No, they'll pass. You know how it is," she said, rolling her eyes as she took a few deep breaths.

Lela assumed that I was privy to her female experience, and I did not fault her for this. Her statement reminded me of the countless strangers in restrooms who'd ask if I could spare a tampon or the feminist-identified male coworker who stated that women were innately stronger because of childbirth or the roommate who asked for guidance about birth control or asked when I last had my period to prove the legitimacy of menstrual synchrony. These assumptions felt like a belonging and a welcoming, but they also felt like an othering. I rarely ever corrected any of these assumptions, because I did not want to be pushed out of the sisterhood. I wanted to belong, so I nodded in acknowledgment, discussed the experiences I had with estrogen patches, pulled out the tampon I kept in my handbag just in case.

But Lela's statement confirmed a suspicion that she was unaware that I was trans. I had never explicitly discussed it with her and assumed that because we were from such a small island, some mutual acquaintance must have mentioned it to her in passing. I knew I didn't want to continue our friendship pretending. There was no universal woman's experience. There were just our experiences, and I wanted to share mine with her. Indeed, I didn't have the energy to withhold from her, and in any case, it felt different with Lela, because we came from the same place and she felt a bit like home.

When we continued on our stroll through MOMA, I decided I'd tell her there. I didn't want to wait.

"You don't know my story, do you?"

"What do you mean?" she asked, sipping her chai latte. "That you used to strip?"

"No," I said, quickly retracing the conversations we'd had as undergrads. She knew that I had worked at Club Nu, and she knew about Troy.

"Well, I guess I don't know," she said.

"I'm just going to spit it out," I began. "At eighteen, I had a sex change, and some people back home know, so I didn't know if anyone told you about that or not."

"Why would anyone tell me that?"

"Well, people talk."

"They shouldn't be talking about *that*," she said, outraged.

"I agree but they still do."

"That's gross. It's no one's business," she said.

I nodded in agreement and smiled through the awkwardness I felt. Lela wore the way she felt like the way she filled in her dark brown brows: exacting and bold. I found myself looking over at her as we continued to make our way through the museum in silence. I wondered what she was thinking and if she thought differently of me and whether what I shared with her would make her limit our friendship.

"I can't stop thinking about something," Lela said. "How did you think I'd react?"

"What do you mean?"

"Like, were you worried that I would be upset or something?"

"No, not upset," I said, "but I was afraid you'd think differently of me."

"Why?"

"I don't know," I said. "I guess it's because not many people know someone who has gone through what I've gone through, so people think we're freaks."

"Do you feel pressure to tell people?"

"Not *pressure*, really," I said.

"Have you told many people?"

"Of course, my family knows and Troy knows, and I told a few guys when I was younger," I said. "But I haven't told anyone in New York besides you."

"I just wonder if people *need* to know. Like, how relevant is it? You're a woman. You're a good person. You're Janet."

"I know what you're saying, and I feel similarly," I said. "I am who I am, but I do feel pulled to share more of myself with some people."

"I feel lucky you told me," Lela said. "But no one should feel obligated to know, you know? It's *your* story to tell."

Lela became my first true girlfriend in New York, someone I could be myself around, because I allowed her to see me in my totality. We grew close as we blossomed from local girls to city girls. I cheered her on as she left the retail floor and began work in the merchandising department as an assistant buyer for a women's fashion brand. The lateral career move also came with a large pay cut. She made thirty thousand dollars a year, something on par with entry-level magazine positions. She made do by working nights and weekends as a bartender at a tapas bar on Second Avenue, which would become our first stop on our nights out.

When she wasn't working, we'd blow off steam at her apartment, which would often be our pregame hangout. We'd start our nights in her bedroom, putting on makeup while listening to Mariah Carey, Destiny's Child, and the Pussycat Dolls. Whenever I hear the Dolls' "Buttons," it brings me right back to the two of us in her tiny bedroom, giddily jumping on her bed while lip-synching the lyrics. We aspired to be as fierce as their lead singer, fellow Hawaiian girl Nicole Scherzinger. Once we were all ready and liquored up, we'd walk tipsily down four flights and head to bars on St. Mark's or meet Nary out in the Meatpacking District. Though we lived a few blocks from each other, I shared her bed more times than I could count. She became my best, most steady, friend—a refuge from my intrusive roommate situation.

Speaking with Mom on the weekends was another comfort. She'd provide me with her own highlight reel of my brother Chad's plays as a wide receiver with the Rainbow Warriors, and relay how she, Jeffrey, and Grandma Pearl would sit in the bleachers screaming and cheering Chad on. I'd tell her about my jaunts around the city with Lela and Nary, about the latest at school and *Playboy*, about the microaggressions I endured with Hazel. She'd end every conversation with an assurance that she was proud of me and was putting a little aside from each check so she could buy a ticket to visit me. I took these as well-meaning, but ultimately empty promises. I had little faith she'd scrape enough together, leave her obligations to Chad and Jeff, and take a week off work to be with me. But she proved me wrong nearly a year into my move.

Mom arrived in May 2006, just in time to celebrate her forty-seventh birthday, with Aunty Lisa who covered their hotel stay as well as tickets for us to see *The Color Purple, Avenue Q,* and *Rent.* I was able to drop my too-cool, I'm-a-New-Yorker front with my mother and aunt and actually play tourist. Their enthusiasm enabled me to look at the city I now called home with fresh eyes. We rode the Staten Island Ferry to get a clear view of the Statue of Liberty. We waited in a long, winding line to ride the elevator to the top of the Empire State Building. We got a glimpse of Julia Roberts greeting fans at her stage door during her Broadway run. We ate an overpriced brunch at Tavern on the Green in Central Park. We walked solemnly around the construction site at Ground Zero, a mammoth, gaping hole where the Twin Towers once stood.

My week with Mom and Aunty Lisa ended with me kissing them

both good-bye on the curb of their Murray Hill hotel. As I sat in my cab, tipsy from one too many margaritas, I leaned out the window and sang "Seasons of Love" from *Rent* loud and off-key. It was me and my aunt's favorite Broadway song: *Five hundred twenty-five thousand six hundred minutes. How do you measure the life of a woman or a man?* Their visit was a well-needed retreat from the loneliness of the large city. It was a reminder that though I could be on my own, I was not alone. I had people, people who may not have had much, but still pulled through to show up for me when I didn't even know I needed them.

ELEVEN

MINORITIES IN THE MEDIA WAS AN ELECTIVE COURSE taught by Professor Pamela Newkirk, the only black faculty member in our journalism school. The weekly lecture used President Lyndon B. Johnson's National Advisory Commission on Civil Disorders findings (commonly called the Kerner Commission Report) from 1968 as a backdrop for examining media portrayals of people of color—African-Americans, Latinos, and Asians—as well as women and gays and lesbians.

The Kerner Commission declared, "Our nation is moving toward two societies, one black, one white—separate and unequal." It also noted the impact the media had on race relations in America: "The media report and write from the standpoint of a white man's world. The ills of the ghetto, the difficulties of life there, the Negro's burning sense of grievance, are seldom conveyed."

The course was a rare and deliberate space that discussed race in our master's program and served as a magnet for every journalism student of color.

So when a six-foot-four-inch white guy, with deep dimples, green eyes, and the fairest skin of them all walked into the class, he was an instant point of fascination. He looked like he had been sketched by Walt Disney himself to save some ill-fated protagonist. Nolan introduced himself as a graduate student in public policy who was auditing the class. What white person takes a course on race just for fun? I was intrigued that he wanted to sit in on a fourteen-week course and listen to a black woman lecture about how mainstream media got black people wrong, and how white journalists and readers were partly at fault. If there was anyone who was an OG woke bae before woke bae was even a thing, it was Nolan. All five of us black girls gave one another knowing looks that said, *Yes, girl, he could get it.*

My crush on Nolan was a passing thing. His hunky presence was the only positive about attending a nine A.M. lecture on Mondays. I ogled him for an entire semester and was struck by how quiet he was and what little space he took up during class discussion. Maybe that was part of his own awareness of his privilege as a white guy? Or maybe it was simply because he was auditing? Or maybe he was afraid to say the wrong thing? Regardless, it only deepened my attraction. We didn't exchange a word or a glance until our final class together. I figured there was no harm in letting him know I had noticed him on our last Monday morning. I let my stare linger. I was daring him to look back. When our eyes finally met, his face lit up. His cheeks flushed red just as I diverted my eyes to the door, which I walked through triumphantly. *Got you!* I thought.

Two weeks later, summer school began. While my classmates took on summer internships, I signed up for a literature course and a journalism class called Writing about Place. These were classes I could have taken in the fall to complete my master's course work, but because I was always in a rush, I chose the accelerated six-week adaptations of both so I could beat my classmates—who would graduate in December—to the job market. In the fall, I would be free of classes and able to work full-time at a paid internship or, better yet, at an entry-level position as an editorial assistant. I regret rushing through my master's that summer. I was so focused on ensuring that I could get a job that I didn't relish the rare opportunity to just be a student. I loved reading. I loved writing. I loved class discussion and learning from my peers and professors. For once I wish I had just allowed myself to relax and take my time.

When I walked into my writing course, I was surprised to see Nolan seated at the long conference table. He smiled and nodded at me as I took an empty seat across from him. It was hard to concentrate on the first-day introductions and the professor's lecture on the importance of place in a story and how we'd be using New York as our very own laboratory. Nolan and I kept doing that thing where we looked at each other just as the other shifted their gaze. It was middle-school choreography that made me giddy. I knew *this* would become a thing.

When class let out around eight P.M., Nolan ran after me on Washington Place to ask if I wanted to grab a drink. It was a warm mid-May evening, one of the first spring days when a cardigan was all the warmth you needed once the sun set. The lanterns and the arch in Washington Square Park cast a dim light on the moving mass of puppies and pot peddlers. I wanted to play hard-to-get and tell him, *Maybe another time.* But I inhaled to give myself a moment to think and was filled with the crisp, clean scent of him. He overwhelmed me.

"Where are you taking me?" I asked.

"Oh, I hadn't thought that far ahead." He laughed. "I'm kind of surprised you said yes. Let me think . . ."

I had flattered him, which pleased me. I had projected Nolan to be some cool guy because he was so handsome, and now I realized that he was one of those rare good-looking people who have no idea how everyone else sees them. We walked in silence to a pub on Bleecker Street, where we settled across from each other in a booth. We dived into our pints of beer to avoid this unfamiliar closeness. He drank an Allagash White, and I ordered a Magic Hat No. 9.

"Never would've pegged you for a beer drinker," Nolan said over the rim of his glass.

"Well, you did bring me to a pub," I said. "Did you expect me to order a cosmo?"

"Very true," he said. "What do you usually drink?"

"Wine, tequila and pineapple, Jack and ginger—depends on my mood," I said.

"What mood do you have to be in to order tequila?"

"A festive one," I said.

"I'm pretty much a beer guy, but I enjoy a Scotch from time to time."

"Isn't that an old man's drink?" I teased.

"Ah, you got jokes." He laughed.

Over the next three rounds, we graduated from flirty small talk to trading the particulars of what had brought us to New York. Nolan told me he was from one of those picturesque coastal towns in Massachusetts, had grown up one of three boys in a family with a "pair of hippies" as parents. His mother worked as an elementary school teacher, and his father was an environmental activist. His parents reminded him and his brothers constantly that their idyllic upbringing near the sea was not the norm for most people. This made him develop a deep curiosity about the world that pushed him to travel. By the time he graduated from Bowdoin College in Maine, he'd been to Kenya, South Africa, Greece, Brazil, and Vietnam. It was in South Africa where he recognized the global impact and universality of hip-hop in places of struggle. While he was there, he decided that he would get a master's degree so he could influence how public schools in low-income communities integrated music—particularly hip-hop—into the curriculum.

I was attracted to the intentionally *good* in him. I asked him to walk me home, and the pink flush returned to his cheeks. On anyone else, his earnestness would have been irritating. On Nolan, it just fit. I invited him up, knowing my roommates were out. I poured us glasses of water, and we sat on the couch. I turned on the TV to give us something to concentrate on before the inevitable make-out session.

The season five finale of *American Idol* was on when Nolan leaned over to kiss me. When I pushed my lips to his, he pulled away respectfully, as if to say, *I just want you to know that I respect you and don't want you to think I came over here just for that.* I wanted him to know that I appreciated how much he respected me, but I wanted him to want me more. So I flung my body at him, pressing my chest against his and placing his hands on my lower back as I kissed his neck. The TV flickered in the dark living room as Taylor Hicks sang that awful victory song all winners must sing when they're crowned. I remember being irritated that Katharine McPhee didn't win. I had been cheering her on all season from my bedroom as Safa watched *Idol* in the living room.

Nolan lifted me by my torso and placed me on his lap. I straddled him, holding him tight between my thighs. I was turned on that he had finally kicked out the good boy. Our lusty bodies pulsed in a coordinated rhythm, emboldening me to slip my hand into the front of his jeans. I was hoping to take stock, but Nolan grabbed my wrist and led it to his chest. The kissing stopped.

"I think I should go while I'm still ahead," he said, with finality.

I peeled myself from his lap, faking a smile to cover the embarrassment of my thirst. Our timing was off. He was careful and cautious; I was always rushing. I walked him to the door and leaned over the threshold, seeking confirmation that things were OK. Nolan kissed me on my forehead. It felt like an act of pity. I went to bed, chastising myself for my slutty ways. The next morning, I woke to a text: *Can I take you on a proper date? Please. Nolan from class.*

He was the perfect first New York City boyfriend. He didn't want anything except to spend time with me. His lack of motive made me trust him immediately. I never kept Nolan at arm's length. I held him close. He was the steady guy you're supposed to marry, whose good-guy-ness was not an act. It was who he was. Nolan became a constant companion, and I spent the entire summer bunking at his apartment in Battery Park, where he lived right by the water and tried to get me to eat salads with him and take long runs along Battery Park. I could never keep up, and he never made me feel bad for disrupting his workouts.

When I look back on that summer, I think about how beautiful I felt walking next to Nolan on West Broadway. It was the chicest strip in SoHo, lined with luxury boutiques, alfresco brunch spots, and people eager to be seen. It was the first time I saw that I turned heads. Here I was, a brown-skinned, wild-haired, ample-busted woman in skimpy cutoffs, holding hands with the tall, blond, green-eyed personification of the American Dream. Out of all the women he was meant to love, he had chosen me. I felt validated in ways I was unaware that I had been craving.

Nolan remained at my side as summer turned to fall, and I graduated from NYU. I did not mark this milestone by walking in a purple cap and gown, because my family could not afford to fly out and witness the pomp and circumstance. It pained me more than I was willing to recognize then that my mother could not make it to New York again for the ceremony and that I would not take part in it, but Nolan didn't let the occasion go unacknowledged. He picked me up in a black town car, brought me a bouquet of flowers and a card, wore a navy suit and tie, and took me to an Italian restaurant in the Village. He ordered a bottle of champagne that the waiter popped in front of us. I can still feel the mist on my skin and hear the fizz in my glass as Nolan toasted me with a raised flute, the golden bubbles sparkling in the dim light.

"Not only are you the most beautiful woman I know," he said, "but you are also the strongest and smartest. I am honored to be with you tonight. Congratulations, Janet."

Nolan was the kind of guy who would make some woman really happy one day, and I always knew that I was not that woman. I recognized it from the start. He was kind enough, attractive enough, smart enough, but he never *moved* me in the way that made me feel obligated to him, that pressured me to be vulnerable. Our exchanges were

limited to the kind you'd have with a great boyfriend but not necessarily a great love. This distinction was part of the reason I remained
silent about being trans, and I rarely, if ever, felt conflicted about not
disclosing to Nolan, a man with whom I shared so much time and
space. I was also still processing the relevancy of my trans-ness to the
relationships I built. I did not have definitive answers then about if
I should tell, when I should tell, or whom I should tell. There were
many other facets that contributed to my identity and experience that
I also held close and could—and sometimes did—share. Nolan and I
were not meant to be forever, so I never felt compelled to show him
that facet of myself.

That fall marked some pivotal changes. I decided that I would
not renew my lease in the East Village. I could not live with Hazel
anymore, refused to take the chance with new roommates, and committed to living alone. It was too soon to even consider making
arrangements to live with Nolan. Plus he had a pretty sweet deal
in Battery Park. The only studios in my eleven-hundred-dollars-a-
month budget were in Queens. Though I mourned letting go of
downtown Manhattan and being in the thick of it all, the price and
the space were right. In the scorching heat, Lela, Nolan, Nary, and I
carried my belongings down five flights to a double-parked U-Haul
that Nolan drove to my ground-floor studio in Astoria. It would
become my first single-girl grown-up apartment.

Nolan helped me make that five-hundred-square-foot studio a
home by playing house with me. We watched television, with me
enthusiastically explaining the entanglements of *America's Next Top
Model* and him trying to convince me that *Entourage* was worthy of
my time. Nolan loved the grocery store and made us underseasoned
pasta dishes—recipes I knew he had cooked to impress women before
me. We had the intimate and close choreography of coupledom down.
He had a drawer that held his spare pair of reading glasses, some boxer
shorts, and other clothes. We sipped coffee while applying to internship and job postings. We spooned into the moisture of each other

after sex. These moments allowed me to forget—momentarily—that I had been here before.

Troy, my estranged husband (which felt like too formal and grown-up a term for our young ages), had a life in Washington State that did not include me, and I had mine in New York. We followed an unspoken rule: Out of sight, out of mind. There were intermittent emails and phone calls—cordial, unemotional, routine checkins to make sure all was well. Troy also deposited five hundred dollars every month to my account. He was adamant about making this monthly payment since the military gave him a stipend for our marriage. It was easy to maintain a respectful distance when distance was all we had. But I was beginning to feel that even though Troy and I were very don't-ask-don't-tell about our marriage, Nolan—who had shared with me the pain he felt after his mother passed suddenly from heart disease when he was thirteen—deserved to know *some* things about me.

I was cutting mangoes on the shiny avocado-hued counters of my tiny kitchen one evening in early October. Just a few feet away, Nolan was sunk onto my brown pleather couch, watching a rerun of *Friends*. It was so domestic. We were acquainted. But there was something about this mundane moment that shook me. I realized I was preparing food for a man I had spent the past two seasons with, but he knew nothing substantive about me. It didn't feel like real life. It felt as if I were playing house in my grandma's garden, acting out visions of possible selves. But I was no longer a kid playing pretend; I was a realized woman with a past, with stories and experiences and things to share.

"I grew up with mango trees on my block in Kalihi," I said, as I held the knife in my palm, slicing through the fruit's yellow-orange flesh. "They were everywhere, but we never picked or ate them. Maybe because they surrounded us we took them for granted. I don't know."

Nolan was listening intently, his ears tuned in to my every sensitivity. He knew I was on the verge of saying something because I rarely offered stories without his probing.

"I never knew how to cut mangoes until a few years ago," I continued. "They're actually super hard to cut, and if you do it wrong, they just turn to smush."

"I don't think I've ever tried to cut one," Nolan said. "I've always bought them sliced."

"Yeah, most people do. My ex actually taught me to slice them."

I had never mentioned Troy—or any man before him—to Nolan, and I could hear his eagerness as he turned his long torso toward me, the couch squeaking beneath him.

"I met Troy when I was nineteen," I said. "He was my first everything, the first person I could rely on. He made me feel safe, despite the distance the Navy put between us. We lived together a bit in San Diego, and when he asked me to marry him, I said yes. It felt like the right thing to do."

Nolan nodded, his green eyes as crisp and sweet as an apple.

"Now we're in this weird space," I continued. "We're married but not together and still in touch. I don't plan on going back, but we feel like this burden, if that makes sense. I don't know. I just felt you should know."

Nolan stood from his seat and reached his arms around me, resting his head in the nook of my neck. "Thanks for telling me," he whispered in my ear, as he stole a mango slice from the cutting board. "I will admit it feels very adult to be your mistress."

"Wait," I stopped. "Is that the right word for a man?"

"Manstress, then?"

I pushed him away, appreciative of the levity he brought to what felt like an uncharacteristically deep moment in our relationship. Once I opened up, it became easy—and enjoyable—to share more of myself with Nolan. I told him about growing up without and how it fueled my desire to make something out of my life. I told him about my nights at Club Nu and how it helped me find freedom in my body. I told him about that night with Anthony in Rhode Island and how it made trust a near impossibility for me. It was my last revelation that propelled Nolan to whisper that he loved me. He looked at me, searching for an echo, for me to repeat his statement. I cared for him, I adored him, but I was not certain that I loved him. I had never lied to Nolan so I burrowed my face into his chest and hugged him as tightly as I could. I knew then that we could not go on, that our end was near. Soon I began dodging his calls and made up excuses for why I couldn't keep our standing dinner and sleepover dates. When I backed out on being his date to his college roommate's October wedding, he finally gave in and retreated.

Soon after my breakup with Nolan, I found myself on another "date," sitting across from Delores, *InStyle* magazine's head of research, who also coordinated the internship program. We were on the eighteenth floor of the Time-Life Building. Delores wore a black circle skirt and a brown turtleneck that was a shade darker than her skin. Her long curly hair was pulled back in a low ponytail. Just as I was readying to go into my peppy two-minute "so tell me about yourself" speech, Delores went into her own monologue.

"This internship is not glamorous. Our interns do not attend events or fashion shows. They do not receive free clothes or products," she said, without inflection. "They have one job: to assist in the publication of the magazine, whether that be running errands, transcribing interviews, or satisfying administrative needs."

I could tell Delores had given that speech dozens of times. She'd sat across from countless intern hopefuls like me who were raised with dazzling visions of what it looked like to work at a magazine, from *The Devil Wears Prada*, *13 Going on 30*, *How to Lose a Guy in 10 Days*, and *Sex and the City*. Delores didn't express pleasure or disapproval. She merely extinguished those expectations. It was the only interview I had where the interviewer did not smile or ask me any questions. Since she headed the research department, I assumed she had already read my cover letter, résumé, and clips and was pleased with what she saw. I could tell she had no desire for me to repeat what she had already read. The interview was more like an orientation, as if I had already been offered and accepted the position.

"When can you start?" Delores asked.

It was Wednesday, so I said, "Monday."

"Welcome to *InStyle*," she said, forcing her lips to spread across her face without revealing her teeth. This was a smile. "I'll show you out."

InStyle was a temp position that paid seven dollars an hour. It was my first, and only, fashion magazine experience. My goal with *InStyle* was to get into the Time Inc. system, which would enable me to have first crack at internal job postings. I wanted *InStyle* to be my last internship and mark the beginning of my career with a position as editorial assistant or assistant editor at one of the sister publications— *Time*, *Entertainment Weekly*, *StyleWatch*, and the publisher's crown jewel, *People*.

On Monday, I wore a crisp white blouse, a structured black skirt from Mango, and leopard pumps from Aldo. Delores greeted me in her office with a fellow intern, who wore faded blue jeans, black flats, a tank that said *QUEENS* in capital letters, and a beige sweater-blazer. She made me feel overdressed, but she didn't seem bothered by my look or her own. Her neutral demeanor made Delores look like a cheer captain.

"Janet, this is Camille," Delores said. "Camille has been with us for two summers. She knows everything about *InStyle* and will show you how we do things here."

"So exciting," I squealed, as Delores took her seat behind her desk and Camille made her way out the door.

"OK," Camille started, as she walked slowly through the hallway. "You're sitting next to me in the Pen."

The Pen was a sectioned-off space in the middle of the floor near the pantry. There were four computer workstations, two on each side of the oversized cubicle. Camille and I were assigned to one side; the other side was occupied by two interns who assisted the interior design editors.

"We don't work with them," Camille said, as she took her seat.

I was surprised that she did not lower her voice. She acted as if they were not there or could not hear her.

The athletic tan blonde, who looked like she had stepped out of an Abercrombie catalog, introduced herself as Kasey and turned to the other girl, a hipster with a jet-black Caesar cut and thick violet eyeliner, signaling her to introduce herself.

"I'm Betsie," she said in a Daria-esque monotone. I could tell that, like Camille, she didn't want to be here, but she at least had made the style effort.

"Nice to meet you both. I'm Janet and so excited that we're all cubby mates," I said, making Camille turn back toward her desk and giggle.

"Our only *real* responsibility is to put together the Sheet," Camille said. "It's a bunch of newspaper and magazine clippings of the day. The editors send suggestions for articles, and we cut them out and paste them onto a broadsheet. We then make seventy-five copies and put them in the mailboxes."

"When do they expect to have them in the mailboxes?" I asked.

"By the time the editors come in," she said.

"And when is that?"

"Around eleven."

"How long does it usually take you to get it done?"

"About two hours, but with us both, it should be half the time."

"So what time do you come in?" I asked, expecting to plan on arriving an hour earlier to complete the Sheet.

"Ten," she said, with a blank stare, knowing that she gave away the fact that she rarely made her deadline.

Camille gave zero fucks at *InStyle*. She did not dress up. She did not engage in small talk. She did not extend herself beyond what she was told to do. She had graduated from Fordham in the spring and spent two summers at *InStyle*, a position she had gotten because Delores and her aunt attended the same church in Jamaica, Queens. It was nice to see that nepotism worked in a black girl's favor. Camille initially thought she wanted to be a beauty editor, because she had fallen in love with *The Accidental Diva*, a witty roman à clef written by Tia Williams, a black beauty editor. Camille had no interest in beauty products, and she rarely wore makeup, but there was something about the way Williams wrote that made her feel seen. She wanted to give other black girls that same feeling, with the same sly, self-deprecating, dry humor. But after two cycles at *InStyle*, she had grown jaded about the publishing industry, never quite believing that it made space for black girls. She was over magazines, over writing, over fashion and beauty, and over interviewing for jobs she didn't want. She was biding her time at *InStyle* until she nabbed a marketing or PR job that would pay her handsomely.

Unlike Camille, I believed wholeheartedly and was deeply invested in my fashion editor dreams, further encouraged by Vanessa Williams's star turn as Wilhelmina Slater, the Botoxed editor in chief everyone loved to hate on *Ugly Betty*. Giving all the fucks there were to give, my first line of business was building a rapport among Kasey, Betsie, Camille, and me. Before I'd arrived in the Pen, the three of them had made little effort to connect, largely because of the fact that they worked for different departments. They spent eight hours together five days a week in a sixty-four-square-foot work space and seldom exchanged a word. To make matters worse, Camille was not the warmest person on first impression, and she refused to code-switch. She treated everyone, from our supervisor Delores and fellow interns to senior editors, the exact same way. They were all met with her expressionless face, a mask she wore to protect herself, one I was committed to cracking.

When Camille first interned at *InStyle*, she was ecstatic until she realized that so little was expected of her. No one was hungry for her witty banter, her creative brainstorms, her out-there ideas. So she shrank into herself, did the tasks required, and spent her hours searching for new job postings in PR and marketing, where she felt her creativity would be valued. When she wasn't applying for jobs, she was writing and editing cover letters and creating handmade thank-you cards that she sent to prospective employers within days of her interviews.

"If they did not remember me in the room," she told me, holding a glue stick and a handful of glitter confetti in her hands, "then they'll never forget me after they open this."

I watched her as she filled the envelope with the sparkly confetti. She planned to glitter-bomb her potential bosses.

"Don't you think that'll just upset them?" I asked.

She rolled her eyes at my suggestion. "I wouldn't want to work for anyone who wouldn't giggle after opening my cards," she said, as she glued her envelope shut.

When I earned her trust, Camille became my unofficial career coach. She'd write me single-line emails whenever she came across a magazine job: *This could be your dream job. xo Camille.* I received about ten of these emails a week, and she would turn to me at our shared workstation and talk to me about how we'd meet for lunch in the middle of the workday once we got different jobs. She'd break down what we'd be wearing, where we'd be living, even our career trajectories and assistants' names. Her imagination was overrun with details. She was visionary.

The first job I applied for that called me in for an interview was an editorial assistant position at *StyleWatch* magazine. I wore my trusty gray Zara sheath dress and leopard pumps and asked Camille for feedback on my outfit.

"You look like a fashion editor," she said, "but you are applying to be a fashion editor's assistant."

"Is that good or bad?"

"Bad."

"Wait! Aren't you supposed to dress for the job you *want*, not the job that is available? Isn't it about showing them how ambitious and polished I am?"

"Sure, but the job you want is to be her assistant," she said. "Not to be *her*."

"Well, I can't change my outfit. This is all I have."

"Just put your hair up, then," she said, and she handed me an elastic band. "Everyone can see you are pretty, but pretty can work both ways. It's safer to be palatable, nonthreatening."

I piled my curls on top of my head into a tight knot, and Camille nodded with approval.

"See? Now she'll be paying attention to what you're saying, not seething with jealousy over your hair," she said. "Good luck!"

On my way to the twenty-ninth floor, I stopped by the restroom again to look myself over. The topknot was cute, but it was not sitting well with me. I felt as if I were shrinking myself, rather than showing up as I was. My hair was clean, chic, and polished. I decided to free it. I did not want to believe that I had to blunt my edges or dull my shine in order to appear nonthreatening. It was a fashion magazine, anyway, and the editor looked glamorous in her editor's letter photo, flaunting long blond curls of her own. And I was right. I killed my interview and left feeling confident that I would be called in for a second one, as well as an editorial test.

When I returned to the Pen the following morning, Camille had left at my desk a handmade card that looked like a Christian Louboutin patent-leather pump. She'd attached a Post-it note that read, *Deliver this to her today! xo Camille.* I hugged Camille tightly when she returned to the Pen carrying the day's stack of Sheets.

"It's not a big deal," she said, trying to contain how happy she was that she had given me something that I liked.

"Yes, it is," I said. "Thank you."

I never got a callback or an editorial test, and I would go in for interviews with editors at *Cosmopolitan*, *Seventeen*, *Nylon*, and *Black-Book* that fall and never receive a callback. It was difficult not to take the rejection personally, and it'd be too simple for me to blame the fact that I didn't take Camille's advice on my hairstyle or that I did not look the part for some editors. One thing that helped alleviate the sting of the consistent rebuffs was contextualizing that I was not alone. I shared a common experience with other aspiring editors—especially women of color—seeking to break into an industry that was not only competitive but also infrequently reflected us.

Minority journalists made up thirteen percent of the workforce in newsrooms in 2006 (ten years later, it would reach seventeen percent), according to the American Society of News Editors annual diversity survey. These statistics, which tally people of color working in newspaper and digital newsrooms, continue to fall behind the nation's rapidly changing demographics, in which a third of the U.S. population is now minority, according to the Census Bureau.

If it weren't for Delores's intervention, *InStyle* would have been pretty damn white. As director of the internship program and head of the research department, she overwhelmingly hired folks of color. She might not have been warm, but she did the work by deepening the bench. Her departments were the only ones that were intentionally inclusive—but interns and fact checkers did not influence editorial coverage. There may have been black, brown, and Asian employees on staff in those departments, but there were only two black women—the only editors of color—who had actual editorial control. There was a senior style editor with her own column who made it a point to walk the long way around to her office so she passed the Pen every morning to let Camille and me know that we were seen. And there was a young beauty editor who walked into the office wearing Louboutins and served dust to anyone who was beneath her on the masthead.

This lack of inclusion seeped onto the pages of the magazine. In 2006, the year that coincided with my internship, not a single woman of color appeared on the cover of the magazine. (The following year, the magazine placed Beyoncé, Halle Berry, and Jessica Alba on covers.) This consistent, systemic erasure of women of color made my dreams of becoming a magazine editor seem impossible. If it weren't for Camille and the crew of young black women interns and assistants we connected with at Time Inc., I would not have built the resolve to hold fast to my dreams.

Michaela, a Spelman College alum, was a full-time freelance fact checker making twenty dollars an hour at *InStyle*. She had met Camille the summer before, when they sat in the Pen together as interns. Her West Coast temperament was easy-breezy like mine, the kind of personality that mixed well with Camille's detached New York girl cool. The three of us had lunch together nearly every day in the cafeteria, where the food was good and subsidized for employees. Listening to their experiences and observations in the workplace pushed me to examine and interrogate my own. Our lunchtime conversations—which we as an inside joke dubbed Brown Bag Lunches—raised my consciousness and pushed me toward owning my particular and specific blackness in ways I never thanked them for.

Michaela, who had attended a historically black university and had met all kinds of black folk on campus, was the most politically aware of our lunch crew. She was also patient with me as I questioned and processed the things they knew to be indispensable truths. For example, once we were discussing the job interview process, and Anika, an intern at *Teen People*, made a statement that she was too dark to be hired as a beauty editor.

"Damn, girl," Michaela said, shaking her head. "Colorism is real."

I looked to Camille to see her reaction, and she continued eating her french fries. I felt I should say something, so I reached for what I felt was an affirmation.

"Kelly is a beauty assistant at *InStyle*," I said. "And she's pretty brown."

"So?" Anika snapped, as she applied another layer of pink lip gloss that was the color of the Johnson & Johnson baby lotion bottle.

"Well, it shows that a dark girl *can* be hired as a beauty editor," I said, looking to Camille and Michaela for confirmation.

"That's *one* example, Janet," Michaela said. "Name another."

I could not name another and realized my mistake. Instead of affirming Anika's experience, I had negated her very real lived experience as a dark girl who had navigated colorism her entire life, not just in corporate America but also within blackness. My mixed black girl self—who was privileged by the hierarchy of the skin-color system— thought I was contributing something substantial by pointing out the exception to the rule. I had aimed to prove that the hiring of one dark girl, one we could count and see, changed the system. It did not. It was not revolutionary to be the only one in the space—that was tokenism. Change comes when the only brings in many more with her.

"Can I be real?" Anika asked the three of us.

Camille and Michaela nodded, and I sat with my head slightly bowed.

"Girl, you will get a job, no problem," Anika said to me, as she grabbed her hair—silky, black, and hanging at an unachievable length past her waist. "You are the kind of black girl who will make white people comfortable. I am not that girl, and that's the truth. Knowing *that* makes me better. It armors me as I walk into these damn rooms, where I am underestimated, expected to hang my head low and walk around bitter. I refuse. *Refuse* to give them what they want. No, ma'am."

I sat in silence for the rest of lunch, considering, processing, and questioning. I learned that there were layers to our blackness, that *we* were not a monolith. We were all black girls, but we came to our blackness and our selves differently. The way my hair curled, the way my brown glowed, the way I spoke and presented—those things gave me access in the media spaces we were eager to be let into. My blackness was seen as less threatening than Anika's. This skin-color and hair-texture privilege was a hard truth to accept, but it was the truth nonetheless.

Our Brown Bag Lunches challenged all I had learned about being the exception. I was taught to believe that as long as I got an education, gained experience, and worked twice as hard, I could gain access. I could be let in. It would take me years to realize that no matter how swirly, curly, and tan I was, I was still black, and my blackness was overwhelmingly seen as inferior, suspect, other. I would have to be over-qualified in order to be seen, interviewed, considered, and hired—and offered half as much. Despite the hurdles, the girls of the Brown Bag Lunch crew were vital to my education and my becoming as a young black woman. They affirmed me, challenged me, and filled me with a greater mission than merely making it through the door. They filled me with an urgency to get on staff and begin influencing editorial content and enacting change.

TWELVE

THE EDITOR LEADING MY INTERVIEW at People.com fought to lift herself from behind her desk. It appeared to be swallowing her. She wore a blunt black bob with side-swept bangs that hung above dark eyes as big as a baby doll's. The heaviness of her blush made her look like a child playing dress-up at her mother's vanity. She sported the kind of outfit that on any other person would warrant a makeunder. A flight-attendant-like coral scarf hung around her neck, and she wore a white tea-length dress and a cropped jacket with big shoulder pads that made her look bigger than her prim five-foot-two-inch frame.

"Hi! I'm Thanh," she said, her left hand extended to me flashing an art deco diamond engagement ring. "Thanks for making time to come up during your lunch break."

We were on the thirty-fifth floor of the Time-Life Building, seventeen stories above my desk at *InStyle*. The thirty-fifth floor was the temporary hub for the new development team charged with revamping People.com, the digital destination for Time Inc.'s crown jewel. It was once the home of *Teen People*, the first magazine I subscribed to.

The hallways were decorated with covers of Justin Timberlake, Pink, Britney Spears, Usher, and Destiny's Child—portraits I'd once coveted as a teenager obsessed with popular culture. Now I stood in the graveyard of my beloved teen mag, which had shut down in September, and I was desperate to be part of its mother ship.

Thanh was a senior editor responsible for developing editorial content. Her latest project had been the Celebrity Database, an online index of biography pages that would improve the site's search engine optimization (SEO). I was in her office to snag one of three temp positions as a writer-researcher. It paid twenty-five dollars an hour.

I walked in certain that this job was mine. I wore a crisp white blouse and black wide-leg pants, and my hair was tied in a low knot at the nape of my neck. After not receiving callbacks for other entry-level positions I truly wanted, I had surrendered to Camille, who advised me to tuck my curls away, leave my chic sheath in the closet, and memorize one-minute sound bites about my work experience, my career goals, and how I could be an asset to an editor's team.

Sitting across from Thanh, I was as prepared as I'd ever be. I'd been on a dozen interviews over the fall, and there was nothing that prepared you more for killing a job interview than actually interviewing. I learned the choreography of it—the easy smile, the enthusiastic nod, the slow and attentive lean forward. I loved the part of the interview when my nerves calmed, we moved past the pleasantries, and I was able to sit back in casual confidence, as if the editor's office were my own living room. But I shone most when I turned the interview into a conversation, asking questions that kept editors on their toes. I learned that I was there to interview them as much as they were interviewing me. The questions that took the longest for an interviewer to answer were my most pointed: "Do you see yourself here for the long run?" and "What do you think I could learn under your leadership?"

Despite the fact that I had a master's degree, two coveted internships under my belt, clips, and solid recommendations, I was still underemployed. I was fifty thousand dollars in student-loan debt, had one thousand dollars in rent due, and about three thousand dollars in my bank account. So when Thanh requested that I tell her about myself, I answered as if my entire future rested on her question.

"I just graduated from New York University, where I earned my MA in journalism," I said. "I am interning at *InStyle* and previously interned at *Playboy*, where I contributed to a ten-part series that tracked male sexuality from conception to death. I have loved magazines since I was sixteen, when I got my first subscription to *Teen People*, *Vibe*, and *Honey*, and by the time I was twenty, I was focused on clearing my own path toward becoming a features editor. I believe this position is a great opportunity for me to learn about the inner workings of online publishing, sharpen my skills as a writer and editor, and give me an edge against my peers by learning how to build a website and structure content for readers online. Plus, I have an encyclopedic knowledge of pop culture and know the lyrics to every Top 40 song since 1990."

"I only know the words to the *Moulin Rouge!* soundtrack," Thanh said with a slight lisp, laughing and exposing teeth that curved forward like a toddler's. "It's my favorite movie."

"Nicole Kidman has never been more beautiful," I agreed.

"I'll be blunt," Thanh said, putting her game face back on as she squared her puffed shoulders. "When I read your résumé, I immediately thought, 'Why doesn't she have a job already?'"

I sat with a furrowed brow, waiting for her to expound. But hers was not a rhetorical question.

"I-I," I stammered, as I figured out how to bullshit my way through this. "I think it's a competitive market in an industry that's struggling to figure out the future of print in the digital age."

"It's an interesting time, for sure. Well, you know this is a temporary position, right? It likely won't be extended beyond March."

I nodded.

"And there's no opportunity to get a byline. It's mostly fact-checking and data entry."

I nodded.

Later that afternoon, Thanh offered me the job through an email from human resources. I gave Delores my two-week notice, and she congratulated me by saying that I could join immediately if that was most efficient for my hiring manager. I was struck by her enthusiasm for my new position, but it was fitting. She had worked with intent to deepen the bench of black girls like me in publishing, so when we actually received job offers, it strengthened her initiative.

The following week, in early November, I joined Thanh's team of five freelancers—three writer-researchers and two photo editors.

Over the next four months, we were responsible for creating one hundred celebrity profile pages to launch in March 2007. My primary task was to fact-check pages written by *People* staff and freelancers and insert the edited text into the website's outdated publishing system. Data entry was the most tedious part of my day, which found me spending hours copying and pasting pages of text, adding keywords, and wearing a wrist brace to protect against carpal tunnel injury.

The job required little writing, but it was better than having to answer an editor's phone, schedule her calendar, and file her expense reports—tasks that I would have been charged with had I been an editorial assistant. Whatever passing dissatisfaction I had about not writing was overshadowed by the fact that my first position in publishing was at *People*, a publication that had enjoyed a marquee presence in doctors' waiting rooms and nail salons since 1974. It was an American household brand, with special issues that had become part of pop-culture lexicon (think "*People*'s Sexiest Man Alive" and "50 Most Beautiful People"). It had spun off successful magazines like *InStyle* and *StyleWatch* and continued to get exclusive features with A-list celebrities. It also did the feel-good "real people" stories that brought readers to tears.

When I started at People.com, though, its online influence was inferior to that of the print edition. It was an unattractive, user-unfriendly website that struggled to compete with gossip destinations like PerezHilton.com and TMZ.com. Its relaunch was a major priority for the executives at Time Inc., who had invested resources into building its presence with a robust new staff. I was thrilled to be a small part of the regime that would rebrand it as "the No. 1 site for celebrity news."

Thanh was an amiable, informal boss, with a knack for oversharing and overdressing at work. Her outfits included whimsical, one-of-a-kind pieces pulled from some vintage shop or an eBay store. She wasn't the kind of fashionista who stocked up on basics—a white blouse, a structured blazer, a few pairs of lean slacks, an arsenal of convertible LBDs. Each piece in her wardrobe made a statement, the kind of garment you could only wear once because everyone remembered exactly where they stood the first time they laid eyes on you in it. She'd walk down the narrow halls, passing our line of cubicles outside her office, and announce to her boss, the head of the website—a short, bald man who wore camouflage cargo pants to the office—the monikers she gave her ensembles. A black and white polka-dot dress paired with black marabou mules was "Minnie at Moulin Rouge." A bright pink blouse with a large bow neckline tucked into a sequined skirt was "Pepto at the Disco."

Thanh's whimsy disarmed people she worked with, making her a collegial collaborator and an easy boss to please. I endeared myself to her early on by consistently completing my workload days before deadline. I didn't want to see work as just a competition, but I figured besting my coworkers's output would help me shine. When my assigned pages were done, I knocked on Thanh's office door, almost daily, for more work. I extended myself and completed tasks that fell outside the scope of my duties. I did so swiftly and impeccably.

I designed color-coded Excel sheets to track our team's productivity across the one hundred profile pages. I answered random hookup facts about celebrities authoritatively ("Yes, it was Brad Pitt with whom Mike Tyson caught Robin Givens in 1989"). I lightened the workload of slow-moving coworkers by reassigning profile pages to myself. I was hungry, ambitious, and eager. I set myself apart by establishing myself as an authority among my coworkers—all young women getting their start in publishing.

I became Thanh's unofficial number two and graduated from fact-checking and data entry to assisting Thanh with her editorial load—editing, doctoring, and rewriting poorly executed pages. My rewrites ultimately earned Thanh's trust, and she assigned me profiles to research and write from start to finish. By March, when the Celebrity Database launched, I had become Thanh's choice for the new permanent writer position, which was announced on the Time Inc. website.

I completed three interviews over a two-week period with Thanh, her boss, and a human resources executive, and spent my twenty-fourth birthday in my studio apartment eating taco takeout Camille brought over as I completed an editing test. It required me to correct a 750-word article, write a 500-word news item, and pitch three ideas for three existing tabs on the website: photo galleries, pop quizzes, and style. I was confident after I filed my test that the position belonged to me. One day in mid-March, Thanh messaged me to come into her office. I immediately began practicing what I'd say to accept the job offer.

"I want to be transparent, Janet," Thanh said resignedly. She sounded uncharacteristically official. "I have to open up the search to a few external applicants. This will extend the timeline for the interview process, and I didn't want to leave you hanging."

"I totally get it," I said, trying my best to assume an unbothered, confident tone, one that would not betray the fact that I was taking her statement personally. I was unsettled. It was difficult for me not to internalize what she was saying as a measure of my aptitude. *Am I not enough?* I asked myself.

"It's just part of the process. This says nothing about the work that you have done here."

Thanh recognized that beneath my cool surface, displeasure was boiling. She understood what it felt like to be rejected, to be told that you would have to wait, to sit in doubt about your own worth. Instead of walking the company line and feigning detachment, she broke away from the role of supervisor.

"You know, Janet," she started, leaving her desk to slide her door shut, "I shouldn't say this, and you can't tell anyone, but I am upset. I wanted to hire you from the very beginning. I thought we'd go through the process and I would make the decision I felt best for my team. I know you are the one, but they don't trust me to make that decision. They don't only doubt you; they doubt me."

I sat with Thanh for the next hour as she told me that she had come to New York only six months before from Santa Monica, California. She had left a position as an editor at an online alternative weekly to follow her fiancé across the country. She quickly nabbed the job at People.com, a career upgrade for her, one for which she was unsure she was qualified. She knew she was a workhorse, that she was creative and affable, yet she still had a nagging feeling that she was not good enough, and didn't have mentors to advise her or tell her otherwise. It was something that had been with her long before People.com, before New York, before Santa Monica. It had been there when she grew up among the all-American kids in Illinois, the ones who looked nothing like her or her Vietnamese refugee parents. They worked several jobs, from a restaurant busboy, to a grocery store stocker, lunch server, and janitor to support her and her five siblings.

Learning Thanh's origin story helped me see the commonalities in our experiences as women of color in America who struggled for place, fulfillment, and achievement in institutions that rarely centered us, from our low-resourced schools to the skyscrapers we occupied.

"HR recommended that I widen the search because they felt you would be a risk for me as someone with little management experience," Thanh confessed. "They told me that you came off as a 'diva'— their exact words—in your interview. I was taken aback by their assessment. It didn't align with your productivity, your hard work. It felt *charged*."

Neither of us uttered the words *racism* or *sexism*, but those words loomed. We spoke in code, because that was what we had learned to do in order to navigate these spaces. What human resources assessed was that Thanh, an Asian-American woman, one so often seen as a hard worker but submissive and not a natural leader, could not supervise—or control—a young black woman. I would run over her. I was told that if I worked hard and did good work, I'd succeed, but corporate America showed otherwise. There was this constant pressure to prove myself, but the moment I did as I was told, "leaned in," asked for what I was worth, or showed confidence, I was labeled a diva. Yet if I didn't excel, I would be overlooked.

We were fighting to be seen as we were while navigating spaces warped by stereotypes that had led the way for us. For black women, Dr. Melissa Harris-Perry has called this concept the "crooked room," where we are faced with the daunting task of trying to remain upright in rooms but are forced to confront stereotypes that portray us as angry or strong (Sapphire), nurturing and self-sacrificing (Mammy), or oversexed (Jezebel). I was attractive and young and black, so therefore HR had labeled me as an incapable, unmanageable, controlling diva who would only dominate my Vietnamese girl boss.

After our conversation, Thanh interviewed a slew of candidates, who paraded past my cubicle to and from her office. It felt like the cruelest endurance test designed to make me doubt myself and second-guess my talents and contributions. I tried my best to resist this challenge by concentrating on doing my job well. I tried to control my expectations. I was entitled to nothing, and comparing myself with others would only hinder me. Thanh and I didn't speak about the situation again, as she did what she was instructed to do and I hoped for a favorable verdict.

On a Friday afternoon, two weeks after our conversation, Thanh messaged me to stop by her office and offered me the job before I could even close the door. She handed me a letter written by the same human resources executive who had believed me to be a diva. It outlined the offer for the writer-researcher position that paid forty-five thousand dollars a year, with benefits, including health insurance, twenty vacation days a year, and a 401(k) that would be fully vested after five years.

"Take the weekend to think it over," Thanh advised with a smile.

I didn't take her advice. I accepted on the spot, without negotiating a better offer, because the salary far exceeded my expectations of making thirty thousand dollars a year as an editor's assistant. This offer seemed ideal. The first person I told was Camille, who had settled into a boutique digital-marketing firm. She hadn't allowed me to second-guess what I had to offer. She'd repeatedly told me that the job was mine and reacted nonchalantly when I sent her messages about the offer.

Told you, Camille replied.

Lela celebrated with me that night at Bloomingdale's, helping me pick out a pair of tall Cole Haan boots and finish a bottle of prosecco at the Burke Bar Café. When I went home that night, buzzed from the bubbles, I called Troy.

"Hey," I said, as I paced my small living space. "It's me."

"What's up?" Troy said in that detached tone he used when he was playing a video game.

"Just got back from shopping with Lela."

"Buy anything for me?"

"Nope. I did get some cute boots for me, though."

"You need another pair of shoes like I need another video game."

"Whatever. These were celebration boots."

"What were you celebrating?"

"I got the job, Troy. I got the job at People.com."

"What? That's awesome!" I could feel his smile through the phone.

"I know. I'm so excited."

"You should be. For real. It's a big deal."

"Yeah, and now you don't have to worry about me."

"I'll always worry."

"Well, now you don't *have* to."

"I'm proud of you. This is exactly what you wanted."

"I know. Thank you."

We sat in silence for a bit before swapping small talk about his work on the ship and the rain he wished would let up. Our call was brief, but it illustrated so much. Troy had fulfilled the role of provider without complaint for much of our relationship, and marriage acted as a glue, keeping us close despite the distance and the obstacles of diverging paths. We could not be rid of each other because we were legally bound. My job relieved us of the burden of each other. The fact that I no longer needed him for my survival in the city freed us. My career would cement our ending, I thought, and I prepared myself to pull away.

A few days later, Troy texted: *Can I see you?*

We hadn't seen each other in more than a year, but I had to admit that I missed him. He was the only man I had ever felt close to, the only man with whom I felt I could be all of myself. I was also eager to show him New York—*my* New York.

I'd love that, I replied.

Two months later, Troy walked into my Astoria apartment and complained about navigating JFK, about the difficulty of getting a taxi, about the traffic on the Grand Central Parkway, about the fact that the buildings outnumbered the trees.

"I don't know how you live here," he said, sighing as he put his suitcase and backpack down. He wore cargo shorts, a gray hoodie, a white T-shirt, and a Redskins cap that shaded his blue eyes.

Seeing him in the space I had created in the city—a space that was now home—I thought of the scene in *Breakfast at Tiffany's* when Doc, Holly Golightly's husband, walks up the stairs to her apartment. He is struck by her slim frame and comments on the fact that no one is feeding her. He then sweeps her off her feet and exclaims, "Kingdom come!" as he crosses the threshold of her apartment. Doc is over-joyed to have reunited with his wife—not Holly but Lula Mae, the fourteen-year-old girl he'd married, the one he called "exceptional," the one to whom he had given a home. Like Doc, Troy did not fit here. And I was unwilling to face the truth that he did not belong where I belonged.

I spent that weekend trying to make Troy fit. I was set on making him love New York the way I did. I took him to the Corner Bistro for a burger and a beer. We ate German chocolate cake from Billy's Bakery. We took a carriage ride around Central Park and got off at Strawberry Fields. I was adamant about forging a connection between the man and the city I loved. I was too afraid that if he absolutely hated it, I would have to finally let him go, and I wasn't ready to do that. Troy knew everything about me. I had relied on our connection as a buffer between me and the world. As long as Troy, the man who knew my truth, was there, I didn't have to open up to anyone else. I was too scared to face myself and be alone.

But Troy barely tolerated New York. It was too crowded, too expensive for him. He was not a city person. He was a man who was clear about wanting a home, a wife, and children. He had no interest in being a rat in this race. I believed that he was irreplaceable. I believed that no one would ever love me like he loved me. No one would accept the things I had told him and still stand by me.

Who the fuck do you think you are? I told myself. *You are a transsexual. You lure men to you under the guise of being a real woman. You don't even tell them up front, and you expect them to trust, love, and be with you. You are a fraud. You have a good man who stayed with you despite your illusions. Not many men would make that sacrifice. He's your only option.*

This was the monologue I recited to myself as Troy held me tightly on the final night of his visit.

"What would you do if I was able to move to the East Coast?" he asked.

"What do you mean?"

"Would you give us another shot if I figured out a way to get stationed closer to the city? I want us to really give it a try this time. Like really try."

I nodded, because that was what you did when someone who loved you pleaded for you. He had never made himself vulnerable or desperate. He had done so much for me over these past five years. He had known me *when*—when I was dancing, when I was directionless, when I didn't know what I could achieve. The least I could do was *try*.

"We can do this," he said. "I know we can."

"Me, too," I said, as he barreled onto my stomach. My hand found its way into his blond hair, both of us lying there as if we had never been apart.

THIRTEEN

THE RESTAURANT WAS DARK, WITH plush burgundy upholstery, bronze textured wallpaper, and gold accents. Ten booths lined the perimeter, with round wooden tables and velvet love seats at the center. It resembled a late-night lounge rather than a fondue place. The scent of grilled beef and boiling cheese threw me as I walked to the booth where Thanh sat. There was an empty clay pot at the center of the table and a full carafe of red wine.

Thanh smiled up at me from her seat. "How great is this? I've wanted to eat here forever. I hope you like cheese!"

Dairy often did not sit well in my belly, but I couldn't resist her enthusiasm. "This is so cool," I said, as I reached for the wine. "May I?"

"Of course," she said, and poured me a glass.

This dinner date had been on our calendar for six weeks, but Thanh had flaked three times. Something always seemed to come up—a last-minute business dinner, an unexpected out-of-town guest. I had stopped expecting it to actually happen. She had first proposed the idea of a celebratory dinner days after I started as a full-time staffer in March. It was one of those impromptu ideas that seemed like the right thing to suggest, rather than something we'd actually do.

"I went ahead and ordered a bunch of stuff for the fondue. Chicken and steak, broccoli, radishes, and cauliflower," she said, as she held a long, slender steel fork. "There's just something about these that makes me feel so sophisticated."

Thanh and I were cordial at work but had not seen each other outside of our office building. She was my boss, and I was her employee, and I was comfortable with those distinct lines. Clear boundaries and knowing my role and where I stood made me feel safe. I didn't want to blur them, especially at work, where the stakes were so high.

"How are you settling into the new office?" she asked. We had moved to the twenty-ninth floor shortly after I was hired, and I sat at a cubicle right outside Thanh's office.

"Oh, my God, it's great. I feel really settled and excited to grow the section," I said, treating this dinner more as a business meeting than as a social call. "I have a ton of ideas for profiles I think we should add. We have a lot of movie stars but seem to be missing TV stars— *Grey's Anatomy*, *American Idol* winners, *The Hills*."

"Great idea. I don't really watch TV, so I definitely overlooked people like that at launch."

We talked shop respectfully, going back and forth about work for the first hour or so, until the wine loosened our grip on propriety.

"Have you ever spent time in LA?" she asked, dipping a piece of steak into the vat of cheese.

"No, but I did live in San Diego for a bit with my husband."

"You are the oldest twenty-four-year-old I know. When I was your age, I was high, riding my bike around Santa Monica." She laughed. "When did you get married?"

"In 2004."

"I bet you were a gorgeous bride. Who did you wear?"

"I wore an Ella Moss maxi dress. It was a city hall wedding, just the two of us, near a marina in San Diego."

"That sounds romantic. Weddings are so much work and a waste of money, anyway. If my parents weren't diehard Catholics, I'd just elope."

"Are you super busy with wedding planning?"

"I am not *that* bride," she said, rolling her eyes. "We got engaged two years ago and still haven't set a date."

I didn't know her well enough to push for more details, but it seemed incongruous that the risk-taking fashionista in our office had not rushed out to buy an avant-garde wedding gown. I could see her in a big whimsical dress with a taxidermy bluebird perched in her bouquet. Pomp and circumstance seemed like her thing.

"I've heard that once you pick the venue and the date, everything else falls into place. I wouldn't worry too much about it."

"Well, I need to get this whole thing going, because I am not getting any younger. Like, my body is changing. What is *this*?"

She flicked the skin at her tricep, which jiggled a bit. Then she raised her torso just above the table and pulled up the hem of her blouse to reveal her midriff.

"And *this*?"

"You are so tiny," I protested. "*Please.*"

"I am not fishing for compliments. I promise. I know I am cute, but this is as good as it is going to get. I am at the peak of my beauty. Eating cheese will not help me."

We both cackled, a sound we produced with little effort. It felt too familiar.

"God, I'm inappropriate," she said, as she took another sip of her wine. "I am your *boss*!"

"Well, we are not at the office." I said, raising my glass to meet hers.

After that dinner, Thanh and I found a rhythm of our own over AOL Instant Messenger, where we corresponded throughout the day about assignments, deadlines, and meetings. She spent most of her workdays in and out of meetings with executive editors about new sections she was planning to build, including a games channel and an online magazine archive. I spent mine in my cubicle, researching and writing new pages for the database and editing pages from a duo of freelance writers we had hired for our expansion. In between talking about work, Thanh and I used AIM to swap links to celeb style photos (she was obsessed with Kate Bosworth; I loved Nicole Richie), celebrity blind items, shirtless photos of ripped stars like Taylor Lautner, Hugh Jackman, and Channing Tatum, and for some extra class, quotes from Oprah and Maya Angelou.

AIM became the platform we used to make each other giggle and swoon, covet and inspire, and it enabled us to build a real camaraderie that surpassed the typical supervisor-employee construct. We became inseparable in the elevator bank, at the Time Inc. cafeteria, the Starbucks in the Rockefeller Center concourse, the smoothie cart on 50th Street and Sixth Avenue, and the New York Sports Club.

The gym became part of our routine after attending an employee health fair, where we learned that not only did we get a corporate discount but Time Inc. also reimbursed membership fees. It didn't hurt that the gym was only a block south of our office. Three days a week, Thanh and I met at seven A.M. to work out together. We did circuit training that I had learned from YouTube fitness videos. I hated the treadmill, so we warmed up by doing sets of jump rope, jumping jacks, and the stair machine. We also did a series of squats, five-to-seven-pound hand weights, and push-ups, which Thanh complained her way through. We then cooled down on stationary bikes, stretched on the mats, and spent forty-five minutes getting ourselves presentable for work.

Our morning workouts made us feel stronger in our bodies and closer in our relationship. We became so much more than coworkers as we shared ourselves with each other. Our conversations then were largely about the crossroads we found ourselves at in our relationships. Troy was preparing to report to his new duty station in New Jersey, and I was torn about moving out of New York City to be with him. It would involve a three-hour daily commute to the office. Thanh was conflicted about her fiancé, the tall Southern man she called the love of her life. He was the life of the party and drank to the point of forgetting their revelries. This had been fun in her early twenties, in a beach house in Santa Monica with barbecues and weed, but at twenty-nine, making him her husband felt like a risk. She craved stability, career, and family and didn't know if he could build that with her.

"Pushing thirty forces you to take stock," she told me one day over the bikes. "If I wanted to smoke and play hostess for the rest of my life, then we'd have a perfect life."

She relayed to me the arguments they had about their stalled wedding plans, about his drinking, about the fact that she wasn't as much fun anymore.

"All we do is work and come home and argue, Janet. I feel like I'm just cleaning up after him and yelling at him about not growing up. We never used to argue. We had so much fun together. We were soooo in love. Like obsessed, all-over-you love."

Hearing her talk about this made me think about Hawaii and Troy and that first year together. It was the specialness of those memories that had solidified our connection. We had never felt like that before, and I didn't know if I would ever have that again. It was the fear of never reclaiming that feeling that made me go back, that made Thanh hold on and hope he'd change.

The first time we fall, we are new to that experience. Nothing can quite compare to it, because you'll never be that young, that open, and that willing. But when you've loved and lost, when you're forced to grow and move on, let go and love again, you become cautious. You learn to protect yourself, to be on guard. You are never as available.

Or that could just be me. I wasn't comfortable sharing myself with people. I let people in with discretion. It took time for me to open myself up. Thanh, though, was trusting and eager. She surrounded herself with people and offered up parts of herself—often intimate confessions that left many with no other choice but to be disarmed.

She wore vulnerability as effortlessly as she wore a tulle ballerina skirt to the office. And so I didn't doubt that if she and her fiancé didn't work out, she'd love deeply again.

Though Thanh was unsure when and if she'd marry, she put her agony on hold to express her enthusiasm for my new beginnings in New Jersey with Troy. Lela and Nary didn't feign excitement for my move. They never told me that New Jersey was a poor choice, but I could feel their disapproval. For them, I was moving backward. Thanh, though, reminded me daily that I was about to build a home, a life, an everyday existence with the love of my life. She made me feel I was making the smartest decision. She helped me feel secure and release any lingering doubt. She'd say encouraging things like "It's only a train ride away!" and "You'll be in the city every day!" and "You'll have a life here and a husband to go home to. How great is that?"

That September, I packed my things, handed the keys to my single-girl studio to Lela, who took over my lease in Astoria, and drove two hours with Troy to Tinton Falls, New Jersey. We rented a two-bedroom apartment in a large complex surrounded by strip malls and the Asbury Park and Long Branch transit train stations. Troy was stationed at a small base in Toms River, which was a forty-five-minute drive from our apartment. Having come from an aircraft carrier, this administrative posting would be a breeze, it offered little opportunity for advancement. This step back was a sacrifice Troy was willing to make in order for us to be together. After all, we hadn't lived in the same city since marrying in San Diego, and it had been nearly three years since Hawaii.

We took advantage of Labor Day sales to furnish our new home. Troy bought an espresso-colored wood entertainment center that swallowed an entire wall in the living room. I decorated it with books and framed pictures, and he beamed when he placed his fifty-inch flat-screen and PlayStation console in the unit. We also bought a beige microsuede couch that felt cozy, and I placed a large wood-frame reading chair that I had always wanted in a corner with a lamp that I had gotten from a secondhand store. We were grown, giddy children playing house.

Troy was my first love, and we were blissful about being in the same place together. We were finally doing right by our marriage, by each other. We were so overjoyed and in love that we could turn every obstacle into a positive. We bragged about our proximity to beaches we'd never visit, about our closeness to everything (strip malls, Red Robin, the Wawa, the gas stations). I used my long train commutes to work as an excuse to read, revisiting favorites (*Their Eyes Were Watching God* and *Sula*), new releases (*Eat, Pray, Love*; *The Brief Wondrous Life of Oscar Wao*; and *The Road*), and autobiographies by senators Hillary Rodham Clinton and Barack Obama. Despite the contentious Democratic primary, I was moved that a woman and a black person were battling it out for the highest elected office in the country. Initially, I doubted that Obama, a black man with *that* name, could transcend blackness and put white voters at ease to elect him as president. I lived too hard a life to believe in miracles, yet still cast my ballot for him in both the Democratic primary as well as the general election. Seeing Obama (a fellow mixed black person from Hawaii), his impeccable wife, Michelle, and their beautiful young daughters Sasha and Malia take the stage in Chicago's Grant Park cracked my jaded exterior. The image of that black family waving in victory made me believe in our collective greatness.

My commute felt like it belonged to a woman with children my age. I woke at five A.M. Monday through Friday to get myself ready for work. Without complaint, Troy drove me to the Long Branch station so I could make the 6:40 train. I got into Penn Station at 8:10, where I'd take the 1 train to 50th Street and walk two avenue blocks, to arrive at my cubicle before nine. I did my work, caught up and lunched with Thanh, and rushed out the door at five thirty P.M. to be on the six o'clock train at Penn Station, arriving at the Asbury Park station by eight, where Troy picked me up, we planned or picked up dinner, and then we had a few hours to watch TV.

In his love letter to the city, *Here Is New York*, E. B. White outlined that there were three types of New York. "There is, first, the New York of the man or woman who was born there, who takes the city for granted and accepts its size, its turbulence as natural and inevitable. Second, there is the New York of the commuter—the city that is devoured by locusts each day and spat out each night. Third, there is the New York of the person who was born somewhere else and came to New York in quest of something."

I had originally come to New York to become someone, but now I found myself as a commuter with a life dictated by train schedules, ending with a bed in the suburbs, so close yet so far away from where and who I thought I was. Before New Jersey, I was on my way to finding that someone I felt I was supposed to be, but I was slowly losing sight of her. When I moved to New Jersey, I canceled my gym membership, swapped long dinner dates with Lela and Nary and Thanh for time-blocked lunches, and gave up direct sunlight—the greatest self-care sacrifice for a Hawaiian girl—by arising before sunrise and getting home after sunset. I had given up the life I had built—for Troy.

I was resistant to the truth: I missed New York. Doing so would have been unfair to Troy, who had compromised his career to be with me. I did not want to look back. I wanted to look forward and hold up my end of the deal. I was committed.

As doubts began to rise, we turned to the things that brought us joy. Troy spent time in the living room playing *World of Warcraft*, and I spent time in the bedroom watching *Grey's*, *The Hills*, and *Mad Men*. We began turning away from each other. We filled the growing void with individual pleasures. We were in a rut, and I didn't want to complain, so I gave in to the idea of finding something we could both like.

One Saturday, a day reserved for errands, I suggested we stop by a pet store in a strip mall we frequented. I hadn't grown up with dogs like Troy, who had slept in a house full of pit bulls. Getting a puppy felt like a promising choice for a young couple looking to build a home, to take care of something together.

As soon as we walked through the front door, we were met with an abundance of cuteness in a gated playpen—a puggle, a yellow Labrador retriever, a Boston terrier, and a black and camel miniature pinscher. Troy bent down to the puppies' level and reached his hand into the pen to pet them. I watched him as the miniature pinscher ran toward him and gave him her paw. She was not much bigger than his hand, and Troy was seduced. Initially, I was dismissive of how smitten Troy was. He had always been committed to the idea of rescuing a pit bull.

"How much does a puppy like that cost?" I asked him, hoping to snap him away. Money talk always pulled him to reality.

He answered by shrugging his shoulders, and I could tell immediately that we would go home with that dog.

"Do you mind if I pick her up?" Troy asked the saleswoman, who nodded enthusiastically from behind the register.

With the puppy in his hands, he looked so happy. The sight thawed my cold front.

"How much is she?" he asked.

"Normally, she'd be a thousand dollars," the saleswoman said, "but I can tell she loves you, so I'm willing to let her go home with you for eight fifty."

He looked at me and pouted, as if he were a boy asking his mother for permission. I knew I had no say.

We went home that day with the puppy we named Stella in a metal crate and a bag filled with toys, dog food, and treats. It was a sweet sight, but doubt soon sank in for me about our capacity to parent a dog. Troy—whom I relied on as a dog expert because of his inability to flip past *The Dog Whisperer*—was adamant that he knew how to housetrain a dog and was committed to giving Stella the attention she required. He was overconfident that he had the time and the skills to take care of her, which comforted me.

We did zero research on the breed but learned quickly that miniature pinschers were among the most energetic dogs. They required
a lot of exercise and stimulation. Troy started out by crating Stella and
limiting the space she had access to. This would help break her from
relieving herself on our beige wall-to-wall carpet. She cried those first
three nights, which lured Troy out of bed in the wee hours. He sat on
the floor near her crate, petting her and holding her in his arms until
she was soothed and he was asleep. By the time I got up for work, I
would be greeted with cold, slushy urine spots.

"What the hell?" I'd scream, half asleep as I made my way to the
coffee maker.

"She's a puppy, Janet," he said. "She's gonna make mistakes. It's
part of the process."

I soon lost my battle with Stella, to whom Troy grew increas-
ingly attached. He'd come home from work at lunch to walk her
and would take her into the office with him. She sat on his lap as
he played video games, and he'd light candles and Febreze in failed
attempts to deodorize the scent of urine that began to take up resi-
dence in our apartment. I tried my best not to complain, because they
were inseparable. Stella was Daddy's girl, and we were happier with
her between us.

Two weeks after Stella's arrival, she began to cough. It was a dry,
rough, consistent cough that seemed too big a sound for a dog so
small. It kept Troy up at night so much that he loosened the grip on
his wallet and took her to Red Bank Pet Hospital. We learned that
she had kennel cough, a condition dogs that have been bred in puppy
mills often get. We learned that buying a dog from a pet store was
the uninformed thing to do, because the dogs likely originated from
inhumane conditions, where they were caged, bred incessantly, and
rarely given space to roam free. It was a business that profited from the
bodies of dogs. We went home that afternoon with antibiotics and a
three-hundred-dollar vet bill.

I was on the couch watching TV as Troy tended to Stella, who lay coughing on a blanket that he had folded just so on the floor. He was seated beside her, petting her. The sound of her cough became so constant that I didn't notice Troy's sniffling. I wouldn't have noticed him crying if he hadn't used his sleeve to wipe his face.

"Baby! What's wrong?" I asked.

"Nothing," he said, shaking his head in an attempt to fling his tears.

"Are you crying?" I asked, incredulous. It was a dumb question that only made him more upset for failing to mask his despair.

"Fuck!" he said. "Shit like this always happens to me."

"Stella's going to be OK. The vet said this is really common."

"Nothing is ever just OK. It's always something."

I could see that Troy, who prided himself on being practical, took each cough as a slight against him, another stroke of bad luck, a sort of injustice.

"Why does this shit always happen to me?" he cried. He sat cross-legged, with his face resting in both palms. He looked hopeless and small.

I knelt next to him to hold him, offering myself as comfort. I could feel the vibrations of his sobs and felt helpless. I tried to be there for him but couldn't help internalizing his comments. I was one of the broken things he had reluctantly grown to love. I was Stella, the girl he didn't know he wanted who turned out to be broken. But he had already fallen too deep to let go. He'd never abandon her.

Troy never spoke about that night. We both pretended it had never happened, but his breakdown nevertheless pushed us farther away from each other. I grew used to sleeping alone, lulling myself with a book or TV. He had always played *World of Warcraft* late into the night, but he stopped sneaking into the bed to cuddle up next to me. He spent most of his nights in the living room, which slowly became his man cave. Alone in the darkness, with Stella on his lap, tobacco in his mouth, a thirty-two-ounce plastic spit cup at his side, and a controller in his hand, he pacified himself. This was his safe space, his refuge. There was no room for me.

"You're addicted to that fucking game!" I screamed from the kitchen one morning as I prepared coffee. He was expressionless, dazed by the glow of the TV. He hadn't slept that night.

"No, I'm not," he said. "It's a damn game, not drugs."

It was easier to blame the game for the distance, for the fact that we rarely kissed or hugged or had sex. The game had become his crutch. He used it to cope with not wanting to be where he was: in New Jersey, at this job, with me. None of it felt like choices he had made. The game, the peeing dog, the train stations all felt like a sentence. We were merely doing time. He was miserable, and I had lost the will to fight. I didn't know how to talk to him without making him shut himself off even more or finding myself in tears.

I had a hard time controlling my tears at work. No one saw me cry more than Thanh during those months. If it weren't for her, I don't know how I would have withstood the gulf between Troy and me. Our friendship survived my life in the suburbs because we saw each other every day at work. During our lunch breaks in her office, I first began to break down and express just how unhappy I was. Thanh was the kind of friend who was unselfish in conversations. She truly listened and didn't have the desire to hear her own voice. She rarely gave advice and only spoke to soothe me with her oft-repeated sigh, "Oh, Janet." It was all the affirmation I needed.

As Thanh consoled me, she was grappling with her own issues at home. Her arguments with her fiancé had become fierce battles, elevated by his attachment to Jack Daniel's and her unwillingness to compromise. She agonized over their inevitable end but just didn't know how she'd do it. It felt as if we were living parallel lives.

Where Thanh soothed me, Lela offered solutions. We maintained our relationship through lunch dates and sleepovers. Lela offered her place as a crash pad on nights when I had to work late. During these sleepovers, over wine and takeout, Lela emboldened me with regurgitated advice she had heard on *Oprah* or from some self-help book. She was never one to wallow. She sought answers. She recommended that

I read *The Power of Now* and *The Seat of the Soul*, the kinds of books I was initially resistant to, the kinds of books that I had long looked down on as hokey or opportunistic. I thought they were merely profiting from the pain of bored, tortured people looking for quick fixes. But I couldn't have been more wrong.

I borrowed Lela's copy of *The Seat of the Soul* and found it quite challenging. It was an intervention, offering me tools that made me look differently at my life and how I participated and contributed to it. It forced me to seek contentment and fulfillment in an intentional way. I learned that no one—no job, no piece of clothing, no man, not even the love of my young life, Troy—could fix me. I had used our relationship as a crutch for years, as a means of proving that I was worthy and deserving. His love was not the solution; I was.

FOURTEEN

THANH AND I WERE WATCHING the Academy Awards on the hardwood floor of her living room on the Upper West Side. It was February 2008. We wore sweatpants and T-shirts for our watch party, sipping full glasses of cabernet. It was a girls' night, just the two of us. Her fiancé was out of town for three nights for work, and she finally planned to leave. It was a day I had never thought would come. Two Sundays earlier, we had been celebrating her thirtieth birthday over high tea at Lady Mendl's on Irving Place. She had seemed happy, blowing out the thirty candles her fiancé placed on her cake. Turning thirty, though, was a crossroads for Thanh, forcing her to make a move.

The next week at work, she told me she had a plan. She bought the boxes from Home Depot, gathered the old newspapers, scheduled the movers, and needed me to help her pack over Oscars weekend.

"I don't know, Janet!" she cried, her eyes swollen from the intermittent sobs. "Am I doing the right thing?"

"Yes, you are," I said, as I grabbed the packing tape to seal another box of clothes. "You're doing this for you."

"I don't know if I can do it. I don't know if I'm strong enough to do this alone."

"You're not alone," I said, writing *sweaters* on a box with a black Sharpie.

Sometimes when you're busy plotting, it's easier to leave emotions out. You're concentrating on logistics and plugging away at accomplishing the overwhelming task at hand. But when you're surrounded by a wall of cardboard and the remnants of the things you collected when you were happy together, it's harder to be assured in your decision. Thanh was not confrontational. She wanted to avoid conflict, so she didn't tell her fiancé she was leaving. Sneaking off into the night when he was out of town was the only way she felt she'd actually leave. She believed that if he were there, he would persuade her to stay, and she would.

"He has no idea, Janet!" she said, as she opened a box to show me a Minnie Mouse costume she wore on their first Halloween together. "Like, I blew him this morning before he left." Thanh had grown up Catholic and confessed everything, even when it wasn't relevant to anyone but a priest.

"Huh?" I asked, thinking she had misspoken.

"This trip was a big deal for him. He's been preparing for this presentation for months, and I didn't want to ruin it with our drama, you know?"

"So you *blew* him?"

"Yeah, that way he felt confident. Was that not right?"

"I just think that because you knew you were leaving, it would be a bit misleading. Like, his last memory of you two together will be you going down on him. How will he ever think that anything was wrong?"

"Oh, my God," she said. "I didn't even think of that."

We both cackled into our glasses of wine. We continued on this way—laughing and crying and hugging and sealing up her belongings—as the Oscars played out in front of us. I was rooting for Ruby Dee, who was up for best supporting actress for *American Gangster* (she lost) and *Juno* screenwriter Diablo Cody, a fellow former stripper (she won). Watching celebrities cry over trophies as my best friend sobbed into her belongings and grappled with the uncertainty of her future was a strange experience. But there was something about the escapism of the Oscars that soothed us both. It made us feel hopeful despite the circumstances.

"Do you think I can really do this, Janet?"

"I do, Thanh."

"Are you sure?"

"I am positive. I know you can."

"But I don't think I can. I don't know."

Seeing her doubt a decision that she had agonized over for years made me want to open up to her, to share with her, to bare myself to her. I wanted to let her know that I knew she could get through this because I was once a girl in doubt, afraid of the unknown, of stepping out on my own. I, too, was unsure whether I could find my own sense of freedom. I instinctively pulled myself back, though, because I feared she would think of me differently. Instead, I put the packing tape down, grabbed her, and looked her in the eye.

"Thanh, trust me, you can do this."

She nodded and chose to believe me. She took the next two days off from work and moved out the next afternoon. She called her fiancé after his presentation in Chicago and warned him that she would not be there when he returned. She moved into a one-bedroom apartment in Astoria—the first she had to herself, no fiancé, no roommates. She was on her own.

That spring, Time Inc. began to rumble with whispers of layoffs. According to media reports, hundreds were on the chopping block in the midst of the Great Recession and a changing media landscape. Because digital was the future, we were not worried about our headcounts—though the promotion I was gunning for would likely not be a reality until the economy bounced back. Meanwhile, my responsibilities at work had grown. I had gone from writing and editing for the Celebrity Database to writing and editing three sections, including the online magazine archive and the newly launched games channel.

During my first review, Thanh, who put on her boss hat, shared that People.com was restructuring and she would no longer be part of the editorial department. She would be shifting to product development. That meant I would fall under the features department, with a new boss and a new title. Though I was sad that I would no longer work with Thanh on a daily basis, I was ecstatic to be promoted to associate editor, with a fifteen-percent raise. At twenty-five, I was officially an editor at one of the world's most popular publishing brands. It was a dream come true.

The glow of my promotion faded when I realized that I had missed another opportunity to negotiate a higher salary for myself. There were three chances to get a significant increase in salary: getting a promotion like the one I had just gotten, using an outside offer to negotiate with your current employer, or moving to another company.

My promotion entailed adding two more sections to my editing duties, as well as contributing to live coverage of awards season, special packages like "Most Beautiful" and "Sexiest Man Alive," and features like weekly quizzes, photo galleries, and tribute pages for fallen stars. The biggest expansion of my responsibilities would come when I was put in charge of the most visible feature on the website, the daily celebrity photo gallery, Star Tracks. It was a slide show of the most recent celebrity images that occupied the front of the magazine and anchored the center spot on the website's home page. The cover image was most often an A-lister or a celebrity with his or her baby. Angelina Jolie and Brad Pitt and their kids, a bikini-clad Jennifer Aniston on vacation in Mexico, or Nicole Richie and Jessica Alba with their kids were all guaranteed clickbait. Still, the website was dominated, as was the magazine, with images and stories of white celebrities.

An inside joke whispered among staff members of color was that *People* stood for "White *People*." I felt a duty to combat this on our website. I had earned access, and my voice was valued, and I wanted to use it to diversify our coverage. I did so by setting expectations with my writers and photo editors, two of whom were black. I used my position as the only black editor on staff to push my photo editors toward greater inclusivity. I required that they show me an array of images that represented many races, sizes, and sexual orientations. (Gender identity was not as much a part of our celebrity culture as it is now, with recognizable trans stars like Caitlyn Jenner and Laverne Cox.) I wanted to ensure that our readers were reflected.

For a black woman to reach such heights was rare, and when we make it into those spaces, we are most often charged with leading the way for inclusive and diverse coverage. I was proud of working at Time Inc., a company that gave me my start as an intern, allowed me a space to grow, and valued a multicultural audience, owning such publications as *Essence* and *People En Español*. Still, I was doing this work with lower pay than my white counterparts—male or female. I resented the fact that I was not being compensated fairly for the heavier workload and increased responsibility. I did not have the luxury to sulk, though. I could not wallow. I could not let my bitterness affect the quality of my work. Doing so would only make it harder for those coming after me. Being the only in the space, I knew my performance would be seen as representative of us all. It was unfair yet true.

My dissatisfaction forced me to properly frame work as work. I could not let my paycheck or my title dictate my self-worth. I could not gain my value from the work I did in this cubicle for this company. I was there to do a job. Though we were persuaded by senior editors to give our all to the website, I knew there was more than this, more than the pile of work that never seemed to reduce, more than the commutes and the silence at home.

I was tired and weary and worried. Parts of me were overwhelmingly desperate to leave Troy in New Jersey, but that faint whisper returned, reminding me of my difference: *Who would love you? Who else would marry you? This is as good as it gets. Who do you think you are?*

When I heard that haunting sound, I knew I needed help. I needed to talk to someone—someone who was not Troy, not Thanh, not Lela. Someone who was not in my life, not invested. I needed a neutral someone, a professional someone.

I sat on a floral upholstered sofa opposite Dr. Delucci, who sat in a recliner the color of whiskey. He wore a sports jacket, the kind with corduroy elbow patches, over a white polo shirt and gray pants. He was six-four, had a gray beard, and dyed his hair black. A wooden coffee table with a box of Kleenex and a copy of *National Geographic* sat between us.

"So what brings you here today?" he asked.

"I need someone to talk to."

"About anything in particular?"

"My marriage, mostly."

"How long have you been married?"

"Almost four years."

"You married young."

"I was twenty-one."

"That's young by today's standards, I guess," Dr. Delucci said. "I got married in my late twenties, but that was in the seventies, so it was late at that time. Most people of my generation got married while they were in college, mostly because, especially if you were Catholic like me, an Italian from Brooklyn, you wanted to have sex with your beloved, so you had to get married. But many of us had sex anyway."

I was surprised that he offered so much information about himself, especially since I hadn't asked him a question. I thought therapists were supposed to listen, nod, and scribble notes.

"Why did you get married?" he asked.

"Because I loved him, and I did not want to lose him."

"Do you still love him?"

"I do."

"Why did you think you would lose him if you didn't marry him?"

"Because he is the only man I loved."

This time, he didn't ask a follow-up question. He remained silent, waiting for me to continue.

"He is the only man I loved whom I told," I said. "Whom I told about being a transsexual. He's the only man who stayed with me."

"I see," he said. "But why would he *not* be with you?"

"Because I am a transsexual. Not many men are into that."

"What makes you say that?"

"It's common knowledge. People think we are unusual and weird."

"Sitting here with me, I don't see you that way, so why do you think anyone else would see you like that? Your husband married you. He chose to be with you."

I was irritated by his sound argument, so I broke eye contact and glanced around his room—the shelves of books, the gilded birdcage hanging in the corner, the boats in bottles that lined his desk. My wandering eyes did not deter Dr. Delucci, who held his gaze until I returned mine to him.

"I guess because he is my first love, and I married him, and I don't know if it's possible to find that again, especially with my circumstances. It's not something I talk about. It's not something I tell anyone about. I am not hiding. I just don't know how relevant it is. I moved to New York and didn't think anyone needed to know, and I just lived, and now I wonder who needs to know, and if they do, what they will think of me."

"That's understandable," he said. "I agree, it is not everyone's business. I don't go around telling people I am on Viagra and insulin, so why do you have to tell everyone your condition?"

"I wouldn't call it a condition."

"I am sorry. I did not mean it clinically. I meant to say it is your business. It's your circumstance, as you say. Your story."

I nodded in agreement.

"What do you do for a living?" he asked.

"I'm a writer for *People* magazine's website."

"I write, too," he said. "What are you writing currently?"

"I write about celebrities for work."

"I mean, outside of work?"

I shook my head.

"When was the last time you wrote just for yourself?"

"I don't know," I said.

"Give it a guess," he said, crossing his long legs, revealing that he didn't have shoes on. He wore furry slip-ons with white tube socks.

"I guess it would be in college. I would write these long emails to my husband."

"Have you ever thought to write your story?"

"I have, but I don't know where to start."

"What about the beginning?" he said. "I've worked on academic and medical books, as well as stuff about my passions, like boats and birds, and I am working on my memoirs. But I think writing, especially for you as a writer, is important. I believe writing will help you process in a safe space. Writing could be good. It could be fun."

I nodded as his eyes drew toward the clock on the wall above my head.

"OK. I think this was a great start. How about we meet next week at the same time?"

When I left his office, I felt lighter. I felt heard. I had never been in therapy. No one in my family to my knowledge had been in therapy. I only knew about it through television, mostly *The Sopranos*. Mental health in communities of color is not a topic spoken about openly, especially in a culture that often pathologizes us. We are more likely to struggle with mental health issues in silence, more likely to go untreated because of shame and stigma. Many people of color wrongly see mental health not so much as a health problem but as a personal weakness, something that a little prayer can heal. But we need more than faith to get us through; we need professional help, too. Just as we seek specialists for heart disease, diabetes, and HIV/AIDS, we need mental health professionals to help us. Grappling with systemic racism, microaggressions, and being the only in spaces doesn't help, either.

I did not tell Troy about my appointment, because he did not believe in talking about your problems, especially with strangers. He really did not believe in concentrating on what was wrong. He felt it magnified despair, caused you to wallow in self-pity. It did not offer solutions. But I had not gone to therapy because I was looking for solutions. I had gone because I felt as if I were drowning and could not find the surface.

My weekly sessions with Dr. Delucci unpacked a lot about my marriage, but we mostly discussed what I wanted to do with my life. How I wanted to invest my time, talent, and energy. Dr. Delucci, who valued self-expression and reflection, continually encouraged me to set aside time to write. I was reluctant to follow his suggestions.

"I write at work all day. I edit everyone's work all day," I said. "How am I supposed to then go home, after working eight to nine hours, and write?"

"Have you ever thought about waking up an hour earlier and journaling? Maybe you can even do some writing on your commute."

This slight shift from *I do not have time* to *I can make time for myself* was the first stage to building a space for writing in my life. I began by purchasing composition books, which I carried with me on the train to Manhattan. I had an hour-and-a-half train ride. Instead of reading the entire way, I wrote to myself.

My early writing consisted of journal entries about the events of the day, how I felt, my frustrations at home and at work. It helped me to process things, to check in with myself. I made a daily appointment to have a conversation with myself. This enabled me to uncover patterns that I could then bring to my sessions with Dr. Delucci.

Initially, I thought that because I was trans and had not talked about it with anyone, my trans-ness would be the root of so much of my therapy. I didn't think that my woman-ness or blackness or Hawaiian-ness would be central. This speaks deeply to how pathologized trans-ness is, how we have learned that we are wrong and that we must be fixed. My sessions with Dr. Delucci were about how I had been living a life where I could not be creative and how my being trans and my past and perspective were not given outlets for me to express myself.

"Have you ever thought that you are a writer who has been silenced by circumstance?" Dr. Delucci asked. "You have been writing for months now, and I notice how much more vocal, open, and aware you are. Do you feel that?"

I never realized that what I needed was a means to express myself. Hearing myself enabled me to heal myself. For so much of my life, I believed that my silence would protect me, that by keeping my circle small, by holding my truth close, by being cautious of others, I would be able to remain safe. But all it did was isolate me and leave me with delusions. I imagined that the people who cared about me would no longer love me if I spoke my truth. But I had to be open and honest with myself, and that began with telling myself the truth: *I need to leave Troy.*

Troy did not allow me to see him fully anymore. He did not openly express any contempt or anger or anguish. He simply disengaged as he fulfilled his duties as a husband. He was settled in the fact that he was doing the right thing by being in New Jersey with me and that these challenging times would pass. But I knew that this would not pass, and I finally broached the topic of our mutual unhappiness one morning as we drove to the train station.

"We need to talk, Troy," I said.

"About what?"

I could hear the weariness in his voice. He hated talking.

"Us. We are not happy."

"I'm fine."

"Well, I am not happy. I feel shitty all the time. I know you do, too."

"We are in a shitty place. It's New Jersey."

"This is not about place."

"Yes, it is. You go to New York every day, and I go down the street to a shitty base in bumfuck New Jersey. You only think of yourself."

"That's not fair."

"Yes, it is. You sit on that train and write in your notebook about how shitty your life is and complain about me and how I don't excite you. Guess what? Life is not about excitement. We are fucking adults. We are married. This is real life, not a movie."

I felt violated but also pleased to hear that he had been reading my journals. *He cares*, I thought. This made me believe that we could turn this around, that there was a way we could make us work again.

"I know it is not a movie. I live it every day," I said. "You are not a victim here. You chose to come here. We both compromised to come here."

"No, I came here for you, and you complain that you gave up your life to be here, and you're an hour away from *your life*, and you complain about how you miss your friends and can't see them and all this bullshit. I have no one here but you."

"If I am all you have, then why don't you talk to me?"

"I am talking to you now."

"I am not talking about now."

"Then what are you talking about?"

"You pick me up, and you play video games. That's my interaction with you. That's my life with you. You retreat to another world, and we don't talk."

"You do the same thing. You read. You watch TV. I play games. Get over it."

"No, it's not the same."

"You act like games are an addiction. It's something to do. It's fun. It's not a disease."

"No, you use it to avoid me."

"Everything is not about you. I play video games for fun. Stop reading into everything."

We sat there at the station in silence for a few minutes until my train arrived. I opened the door to step out of his truck.

"I love you," he said.

"Me, too."

I boarded the train, knowing that I would not be doing this for much longer. It all felt like a transaction. On one side was life—New York, my friends, my career. On the other side was Troy. He began to feel like an obligation, something I had to do, something I had to travel to. It felt as if I were doing time because he was the only person to accept me, love me, and stay with me. He deserved more than that. He deserved to be in *life* with someone. We were broken. We disappointed and hurt and betrayed each other, and New Jersey was our way of trying to salvage what we remembered we once had together. The beaches of Waimea were so far away.

When I relayed the conversation to Dr. Delucci that week, he suggested that I write Troy a letter, since our conversations so often turned combative.

"You don't have to send the letter," he said. "Just write it for yourself. That way, when you talk again, you will have processed your feelings."

I worked on the letter for two weeks and left it on the console of his game player, near the power button, where I knew he'd see it.

Dear Troy,

I am writing to you because we no longer know how to talk to each other, when all we once had was our conversations on the phone, through our emails. I know you always said I just talked at you and you listened, but now we don't even do that. So a letter is the only way I can be clear about what I feel without yelling or crying.

We are not who we were to each other. We are not kind. We do not listen. We can't even have a conversation. I cannot live like this, and I know you can't, either, but you will because you made a commitment. I don't want to speak for you, so I will speak for myself.

This is not working for me, and I don't want us to sit and fester and resent each other. You say you came here for me, and this hurts, because I know we both came here for the possibility of us finally doing it right. We came here to give our marriage a real chance at working. But it is not working.

It seems ridiculous to say, "We need space," when all we once had was space, but I feel it's the right thing to do. I have to leave.

Love, Janet

Troy never mentioned the letter when he dropped me at the train station. He never mentioned the letter when he picked me up. He never mentioned the letter when we picked up pizza. He remained silent, as if to call my bluff, as if ignoring it would make it go away.

A week later, Lela drove to New Jersey with Thanh in a rental car that Thanh had put on her credit card. I planned to stay with Lela in the Astoria apartment that I had once called my own. She was planning to move back to the East Village in a month, and I would take over the lease. The three of us loaded the trunk with my clothes, toiletries, documents, and notebooks. I sat in the backseat next to the reading chair I loved so much, with a box of tissues that Thanh had thoughtfully brought.

I, too, expected to be inconsolable, sobbing to the point of dehydration. I was melancholy about this ending, disappointed in myself for not staying longer than seven months, frustrated that we did not have the tools to make us work. I played out his return home that evening. I wondered if he'd even notice my absence—the empty drawers, the missing chair. Would he be angry? Would he be despondent? Would he convince himself that I'd return?

I would not witness that scene, and he would never share how he felt in my absence. When we did talk, he only asked when I'd be back. He saw my leaving not as an exit but as a temporary matter, something I had to do out of convenience. Troy was in disbelief. It was easier to blame New Jersey and the commute rather than look at us. He delayed our farewell by believing I'd come back home to him and Stella. But what we defined as home had long shifted. We no longer defined it as where the other was.

After two hours, we neared the Lincoln Tunnel and dwelled in traffic on the cement helix. The Hudson River wore a shiny navy blue that matched the backdrop of the Manhattan skyline. The glittering towers and illuminated windows twinkled in the dusk that held us. It was a vision glowing through the oncoming dark—so reassuring, so welcoming, so majestic. It moved me to tears.

I had seen the skyline countless times—from the Williamsburg Bridge, the subway tracks in Astoria, the twenty-ninth floor of the Time-Life Building. But this time was different. This time, each burning light in each pillared structure, like a lighthouse incandescent and unmoving in the dark, signaled some meaning. It told me I belonged. I was home.

FIFTEEN

IT WAS STRANGELY FREEING TO BE ALONE, to not be obligated to anyone but myself. I didn't have to *do*. I didn't have to speak. I merely had to *be*. I thrived in solitude. I was grateful to have the space to mourn what Troy and I once had, to deal with the heartbreak and pull myself back together. I had a hard time forgiving myself and getting over the guilt.

I was haunted by the image I had of Troy alone in the apartment we had furnished together, a home he had not chosen, a home he had made because of me. We lived together for seven months. That's all the time I could do in New Jersey with him. He still had another two years at his duty station, a place where he felt underutilized. I tried not to think too deeply about his pain or struggle, because I was faced with the hardest work any person has to do: facing myself.

I sat in that apartment alone and reconnected with myself by taking Dr. Delucci's advice. I wrote in my journals before work. I would not call the writing literary, but it was self-revelatory, enabling me to tell myself my own stories, stories I had kept tucked away for so long.

"All artists, if they are to survive, are forced, at last, to tell the whole story, to vomit the anguish up," James Baldwin said. His words were a salve, encouraging me to tell myself stories. These writings—some fiction, some memoir—gave me a chance to give testimony to where I had been. For so long, I had believed that pretending I had come from nowhere would protect me, save me.

My salvation began on those pages. They remain the roots on which I stand now, pushing me to prioritize myself, my thoughts, my growth. I took my NYU professor's advice, too, and began using the city as a laboratory. I attended public talks at colleges, bookstores, and the Kabbalah Centre. I watched *Rent* five times in its final year on Broadway. I signed up for a writing course in NYU's continuing education program. I sweated it out during boot camp classes at the New York Sports Club, with Thanh breathing heavily at my side.

Thanh became a constant in my life, a sister-friend with whom I could giggle and grow, a woman who was present through the tears and cheers, eager to show up in ways no one really had in my life. Our workouts, red wine binges, and brokenhearted single-girl sleepovers led to countless moments of self-revelation. We solidified deep bonds that led me to realize that shielding myself from Thanh was unnecessary. She would remain. I called her one afternoon before a dinner date to finally tell her my story, to let her see me in my totality.

"I need you to know that I've wanted to share something with you many times, but I was scared," I said, pacing my apartment, a bit shaky and uncertain.

"Don't be scared," she said in her reassuring way. "It's *me*. There's nothing you could do that would make me not love you."

After I opened up to her, she breathed a sigh of relief and scolded me.

"You acted as if you murdered someone or something. My God!" she shouted before cooing, "Janet, I love you. You are exactly who you are supposed to be."

Despite the friendships I was forging and the time I was investing in myself, I could not break away from Troy, who would insert himself into my life by being resourceful. He felt that if he could prove to me that I needed him and what he could provide, then I'd come back. He'd drive to the city using the belongings I left behind as an excuse. He could have easily loaded up his truck with my personal items and delivered them in one trip. Instead, he turned this task into a series of trips, giving him a reason to see me and check up on me. He'd stop by with drugstore items (toilet paper, cleaning supplies, lotion) and gifts I didn't ask for, like the Kindle he bought me for my twenty-fifth birthday, just weeks after I left him.

It was difficult to accept his kindness. His gifts made me feel obligated to him. I was working hard to release myself from the burden in my sessions with Dr. Delucci. When I'd protest about Troy's generosity and his need to provide for me, Troy would remind me of our roles: "You are my wife. I'm *supposed* to do this."

I was not brave enough to tell him to stop, to tell him not to come over, to tell him that I would not be coming back, to tell him that I wanted and needed a divorce. Instead, I tried to soothe him. I cared about him, and I wanted him to be happy, and I felt guilty for leaving him behind. I knew that the solitude that helped me thrive felt like a forced sentence to him. It wasn't as if he wanted *me*. Like so many of us, he just did not want to be alone.

Troy persisted for the next two years. The fact that I began dating again did not deter him. The fact that I had met a man named Aaron in a Lower East Side bar did not deter him. The fact that Aaron and I were getting serious did not deter him. He was confident that if he continued to show up for me, I would come back to him.

I remember the day when he finally let go. It was June 2010, and I was sharing an apartment in the East Village with Aaron, whom I had been dating for a year. That weekend, we were hosting my brother Chad and his future wife, Jane. It was Chad's first trip to New York City, and Troy, with whom I had remained in contact mostly through email and calls at my office, used Chad as an excuse to check Aaron out.

Troy and I were playing this game where we believed the illusion that we could just be friends and remain in each other's life. Aaron, being a *real* adult, did not like the game. He thought it was dangerous. Still, Troy was adamant about taking Chad out to lunch, and I didn't see the harm. They had a good relationship but were far from close. Chad was always grateful that I had Troy. His sister's being in a relationship meant safety to him. He often worried that me being out there single and dating meant risk, that someone would hurt me.

Initially, we planned for Troy to go to lunch with Chad and Jane, but our lunch ended up being a packed affair, where Troy would be meeting Aaron. I chose Cafecito on Avenue C, a small Cuban restaurant around the corner from our apartment. When we walked in, Troy was seated at the bar, with a Corona in hand. Chad walked in first, with Jane at his side. Troy and Chad shook hands and hugged. Troy kissed Jane on her cheek, like we do in Hawaii. I walked up and hugged Troy, and he held for a beat too long. Aaron stood at a respectful distance. When Troy let me go, he zeroed in on Aaron and made the first move.

"Hey, man." He greeted Aaron, reaching his hand across us. "Nice to meet you."

"It's a pleasure," Aaron said. "I've heard many great things."

Aaron was performing full Midwestern charm for Troy, the way he put people who would be intimidated by his height, his handsomeness, his blackness, at ease. He was practiced, I would later learn. His charm brought Troy in and extinguished the awkwardness that Chad, Jane, and I were feeling with the exchange.

We were seated at a rectangular table bordered on its long sides by benches, with sole chairs at either end. Chad and Jane shared a bench, I sat opposite them on the other bench, and Troy and Aaron sat at opposite ends, facing each other across the table. Most of the conversation was catching up among Chad, Troy, and me, while Jane and Aaron listened respectfully for a bit before having their own conversation outside of our trip down memory lane. It was cordial, and I pretended that it was not bizarre that the man I was divorcing, with whom I had spent the past seven years, was having lunch with the man I knew I could someday marry.

Aaron and I were starting a life together, and we had a home together—and Troy was persistent in maintaining a connection with me. I rarely mentioned Aaron during our calls, but Troy knew when I slipped and said *we* when it no longer meant Troy and me. Aaron was like the man no one spoke of but who hovered over our conversations, and I felt I was being respectful by not throwing his presence in Troy's face. I was protecting him from heartache, but all I did was obscure the truth: I had moved on, and I was tolerating this connection out of obligation and duty to our shared history. It was pity. No one should be pitied, and Aaron knew that.

Troy was obstinate when the check came, and Aaron pushed back respectfully to cover lunch. I suggested we split it, but Troy was unmoving.

"Let me get it," Troy said. "I wanted to take Chad out."

Aaron nodded in defeat and thanked Troy—we all did.

Aaron and I led the way out of the restaurant, and Chad, Jane, and Troy trailed behind us. As we neared parting at Avenue B, Aaron reached his arm around my waist and did not let go. This was the way he held me, making me feel protected and petite. But his embrace felt like a betrayal. I wanted to pull away from him, but Aaron maintained his grasp. I would be angry with him for months for that show of affection, but he pushed back.

"He needed to know that I had you, that it was time for him to go," Aaron told me.

Aaron did not mean *had* as in *possession* but *had* as in *I've got her. You don't have to worry. I'll take her from here. There's no more for you to do here.* Troy was behind us, watching the woman he loved settle into the arms of another man. He was forced into a realization that I was no longer his. I was hyperconscious that Troy was watching and aching. This touch broke the agreement that we had silently made to each other to keep pretending and prolonging something long broken.

Chad, Jane, and Aaron said their good-byes to Troy at the corner, as I walked Troy to his truck.

"Thanks for lunch," I said, as he opened the passenger door and handed me some CDs and DVDs he had finally separated from his collection.

"Yup," he said. "This is the last of it."

I reached my arms out to grab the bag from him, and he began to sniffle. He held his head low, his cap shielding his eyes.

"Troy . . ." I said, reaching for him.

He pushed my hand away. "Stop. I'm OK."

"I'm sorry."

"Just go," he said, shutting the door. "Go."

I followed him to his driver's-side door, and he kept telling me to go. He said he didn't want my pity. But I knew then that he really loved me and was mourning a loss, something I had mourned already and had let go. I grabbed him and held him in my arms. He was reluctant until he wasn't. He cried, and I rubbed his back. We stood that way for five minutes. This was our good-bye.

He drove off on 13th Street toward Avenue A, and I never saw him again. He would push forward the divorce papers I had prepared online months before, and we coordinated through email without attorneys. I was adamant that Troy file, because I wanted him always to be able to tell the people in his life that he had ended it. With the writing I was doing, I knew that someday I would share my experience publicly, and I wanted Troy to say what he felt he needed to say. He told me he didn't care what people thought. "It's no one's business," he said.

I appreciated his protest, but I wanted to give him the one thing I knew I could give him: an out. He could claim that he didn't know, that I had withheld my story from him throughout the relationship, the way I've heard some women have, women who lived *stealth*, who told their husbands that they'd had hysterectomies and lived in fear of being found out. Their white picket-fenced bliss, complete with adoptive children, a loving spouse, and PTA meetings standing on the wobbly foundation of truths withheld. I wanted to protect him, because I knew that he came from a conservative small town, that he was in the military, that masculinity was fragile. I didn't want people to judge him, to judge us.

We cited irreconcilable differences. He kept the furniture and his truck, and I kept my student-loan debt. By the end of the year, we were unbound. Law no longer held us to be accountable to each other—it was an ending and a freeing.

"You finally made an honest man of me," Aaron joked when I shared the news with him. "Do you know that I had two requirements for my dream woman?"

I shook my head.

"I wanted her to be from Hawaii," he said. "And I wanted her to have been married before."

"Really?" I asked, incredulous.

"I'm serious. I wanted a woman who knew what marriage was really about. Not a wedding but an understanding that marriage is work and that sometimes we fail."

Aaron always knew how to make me feel better about my life choices—experiences that would be a cause for concern for any other man. I couldn't shock him, and that was comforting for a woman who seemed to steadily have *something* to reveal. We found our own ways as a couple living together in the East Village. The newness of our relationship made it easier to move on, to forget, to erase the fact that I had done this before. I had bought furniture with someone before. I'd had conversations about what to eat with someone before. I had scolded a man for using too many sheets of paper towels before.

What I hadn't done before was be completely honest and open and trusting. With Aaron, I didn't hold tightly to myself. I wasn't as fearful about sharing myself, emotionally and physically. A lot of this had to do with maturity and experience. I was at a point in my life where I was ready and willing to open up and talk, and we did this well together. Aaron was a generous, affirming listener, who encouraged me to keep writing about myself. He was by my side—a steady, close presence—when I made the decision to step forward publicly for the very first time.

It was late 2010, and the article in which I would open up about my journey to womanhood was scheduled to come out in May. I had already told some people I was close with—Thanh and my family—about the impending article, but I hadn't yet spoken to Troy. I decided it was OK to break our code of silence, which allowed us to move on with our lives. I sent him a short email detailing my plans for publication. He replied with one line: *I'm happy for you.*

The last time we spoke was over the phone in May 2011, after he read my *Marie Claire* article in a local bookstore. The image of him standing in the magazine section of a Barnes & Noble and reading an article in a fashion magazine about his ex-wife's transition made me a bit uneasy. It didn't seem right. Many of the details in that piece would be new for Troy. I should have told him those things in person, but he wasn't someone who had prodded me with questions when we were together. For him, the past was past, and he kept it there. But we navigated the awkwardness of the situation respectfully during our phone call.

"I just read the article," he said. "You looked beautiful."

"Thank you," I said. "What'd you think?"

"It was good," he said. "Made me sad, though."

"Why?" I asked.

"I just didn't know a lot of those things," he said. "I wish I knew, you know?"

"Yeah, I should've told you," I said. "I'm sorry."

"No, it's not your fault," he said. "I blame myself, I guess. I didn't know if it was OK to ask, so I never did."

He paused, and I could tell he was thinking of what to say.

"I wanted to know," he continued. "I want you to know that I *wanted* to know."

"I appreciate that," I said. "But I was happy that you didn't ask then, because I don't think I was ready to tell."

"I guess that makes sense," he said.

He paused again, and this time, I knew it was time for me to move us along. "I'm glad you read it," I said. "I have a meeting now and should probably go."

"Me, too," he said. "Probably should buy a book or something before I leave."

"I know, right?" I giggled. "It was good talking to you, Troy."

"It was," he said. "I am proud of you."

When we hung up, I was struck by how the *we* that we had invested so many years in had been publicly erased. More specifically, I had publicly erased Troy. I never mentioned him in that article or any other essay I wrote. In *Redefining Realness*, I omitted him, out of respect for his privacy but mostly because of the strength of the narrative. I preferred to present the portrait of a woman who had never had love, who had never been experienced, who was untouched until *true* love arrived. As a writer, it was the line of a stronger desire, one that offered simplicity for the reader.

But love is not simple. It's messy. Love forces you to face yourself and grow up. That's what I had with Troy. It was as true as anything else I had experienced. He was the man who saw me when I was "in process." He was the guy who met a pretty young girl in a strip club when she was still covered in secrets. Despite any reservations or what anyone thought, he stuck by her as she figured herself out. He stood witness to my becoming, and as much as this book is an ode to my younger self, it is also an ode to him—the first person to stand by my side and love me.

We couldn't make forever, but forever isn't love's sole ambition. The goal is to be impacted, to be changed forever. Troy influenced me and is imprinted in me, and I believe I am imprinted in him. I will never look at Waimea Bay the same way, and I no longer dismiss the talent of Dave Matthews, and I can't bite into an *ahi poke* roll without thinking of Troy's face. Troy was a constant, quiet force, who always showed up when I needed him during those pivotal years when I was most doubtful and insecure about my abilities and myself. He was confident enough to show up for both of us, the first person to do so for me. Because of his presence in my life, I grew confident and steady in myself and began to believe.

That belief enabled me to move on and away from the home I had with him and to find myself in New York City and share myself again with someone else. I married Aaron in a beachfront ceremony on the North Shore in 2015.

Troy also got married again. I cried when I saw a photo of him, beaming next to a chubby-cheeked baby who had his big blue eyes, my favorite feature of his. It was comforting to see that we both got what we wanted, and this was genuine happiness. Our love felt like a growing thing, something that allowed us to meet and share and mature to a point where we moved beyond each other and ourselves. We grew too big, loomed too large, and sought other spaces. We left each other, but the love remains.

AFTERWORD

AARON AND THANH WERE ADAMANT about throwing me a thirtieth birthday party. They saw it as their duty as the thirty-somethings who were closest to me. I resisted the idea as soon as it was proposed.

I hated parties, and I loathed crowds. My easy smile, gregarious nature, and love of the camera deceives many into believing that I am a social person, an extrovert. I'm good with people. I genuinely like people. But I'm also a great pretender, who tolerates the company of others. It took me years to come to terms with the fact that I preferred solitude over soirees.

Coincidentally, it was a discovery I made just as my work, my writing, and my life attracted an audience after I told my story publicly for the first time in 2011. The more known I became, the more I craved the comfort of home—a book, my television, and my computer. Reading, writing, and bingeing were tasks that required me to be with myself. It was the company I learned to crave most.

I'd now yielded to the fact that I no longer existed in isolation. I had a community of people who loved me and cared for me and were eager to celebrate this milestone with me. I was obligated to them, as much as they were obligated to me. So I borrowed a black leather dress from Wendi, my longtime best friend who had moved to New York just a year before. I approved the table tents and posters Thanh had gleefully designed to personalize the bar. I nodded when Aaron asked if I'd be OK with a DJ and a drag queen performance. I taste-tested the delicious German chocolate cupcakes that Lela prepared.

On a chilly night in March 2013, I took a deep breath as I walked down the steps of that Union Square club to the private basement bar Aaron had rented. I had already rehearsed the small talk I'd be forced to have with my guests' plus-ones. I had already taken two tequila shots to steady myself as I grew anxious about greeting the 120-plus people, from longtime friends and acquaintances to former colleagues. I had already designated the good side from which I would take countless selfies, dictated by the side part I wore in my curls, which had grown wilder and fuller over the years.

As I reached the bottom of the stairs, I was ready to make my entrance. It was nine thirty P.M., and the room seemed hushed. I was afraid no one would show up. When I rounded the corner toward the entryway, I saw Aaron taking a photo of Nary and his girlfriend. I saw Lela and her boyfriend placing her cupcakes on a tiered gold stand as Camille art-directed. I saw Thanh, who had gotten married the year prior, arranging table tents and streamers at the long wooden bar with her husband. I saw Leo, my friend from Rhode Island, helping the DJ—an artist he managed—set up the booth.

There were only about ten people in the room, which was lined with leather booths and strobe lights. I silently watched them fussing about for a minute without being noticed, and I realized I had arrived a half hour early. The sight of them busying themselves to make the room just right for my arrival showed me what love looked like. As I'd resisted the idea of this party, I hadn't given myself a chance to recognize that I wouldn't be celebrating with just any crowd. It wasn't another college auditorium where I took center stage at a podium or a camera-phone-clad line of readers eager for a selfie and personal inscription.

This was *my* crowd. I had chosen these people. They *knew* me, *saw* me, *loved* me.

I couldn't have mapped out a more ideal entrance than this room full of people who were the first to make me feel secure enough to truly *be*—without evading or hiding or wearing that cloak of normalcy I had held on to for most of my twenties. They were my first audience, my first readers, my first champions. They were the ones who were there before the world knew my name. They knew me *when*.

As I announced myself to that dim, decorated room, I kissed the man who would become my husband and hugged my best friend and thanked them both for forcing me to take a moment to reflect and celebrate. Their care reminded me that I didn't *always* have to be on one hundred. I could chill and laugh and drink and dance, even with a Beyoncé impersonator in a sickening blond lace-front, until I split the hem of my skintight skirt. I could drink until the room spun. I could come to grips with saying good-bye to a formative decade full of several pivotal firsts—my first love, my first college experience, my first apartment, my first real job, and, most important, my first step toward taking ownership of myself and my story.

My twenties represented a time when I had no other obligation than to figure out who I was. I took the time I needed to just *be*—to learn how to advocate for myself before becoming an advocate for others. I was accountable to myself. It was a time for me to process the experiences that had shaped me and to be bold enough to seek new ones. It was a time for me to make mistakes and learn from them. It was a time for me to seek my voice, my purpose, and my place in the world. My twenties taught me to create and uphold much-needed boundaries, to take hold and possession of my body, and to stake a claim on my life. My twenties also taught me to improvise and to loosen up. Boundaries are vital, but at times I could be unmoving about these self-imposed restrictions, and that often prevented me from going where I truly wanted, from knowing others as I wanted to be known, from loving and being loved in the way I desired.

My twenties prepared me to be *seen* fully—in my own eyes, in the eyes of the people I know and love, and in the eyes of the public I've invited into my life to know me. More than anything, it was my act of being *in process* during those messy, fun, and formative years—all the decisions and mishaps, all the highs and lows—that brought me to yet another dark room. This time, though, I was free, overwhelmingly secure in who I was and certain that she was—and would be—enough.

ACKNOWLEDGMENTS

GRATITUDE IS A PRACTICE THAT RECOGNIZES one's smallness and interconnectedness. None of us—no matter how isolated we may feel—achieve it all alone. Thank you to the following for conspiring with me: My editor Rakesh Satyal, whose intelligence, wit, and incisive feedback improved this book. The folks at Atria Books for championing my memoir—especially Judith Curr and Peter Borland.

My agent Ryan Harbage, who advocates for me and my creations. Sarah Branham, my first editor, for making this memoir your final acquisition. I couldn't have written it without your belief that I had something else to say.

My residencies at Hedgebrook gave me serene space to struggle through this manuscript. Thank you for nurturing women writers from all walks of life.

This memoir centers my remembrances of many pivotal moments—some of which were shared with people I love. Thank you for allowing me to betray you by telling my version of our history: my parents and siblings; Charlise, Diane, Ed, Kristina, Mai and Nary; and long-lost friends and lovers—especially the one who cannot be named. You'll always be my first.

Finally, Aaron: Thank you for having vision, for seeing me before I could *fully* see myself, and choosing to be in *life* with me.

ABOUT THE AUTHOR

JANET MOCK IS A WRITER, TV host, and advocate whose work has appeared in the *New York Times*, *Marie Claire*, and *The New Yorker*. With a master's in journalism from New York University, the Honolulu native began her career as an editor at People.com. In 2014, she released the groundbreaking and bestselling memoir, *Redefining Realness*, about her inspiring story of growing up as a transgender girl.

Since then, Janet has become, as Oprah Winfrey said on OWN's *SuperSoul Sunday*, a "trailblazing leader" championing the rights of America's marginalized, including trans people, women of color, and LGBTQ youth. A sought-after speaker, she gave a rousing speech at the Women's March on Washington, and her work has been honored by the Ms. Foundation for Women, GLSEN, Planned Parenthood, and the Sylvia Rivera Law Project. *Time* called her one of "the most influential people on the Internet" while *Fast Company* named her one of the "most creative people in business."

Janet tells stories across many platforms: she produced the HBO documentary, *The Trans List*, served as a correspondent for *Entertainment Tonight*, hosted a series of television specials, including the digital talk series "So POPular," MSNBC's "Beyond My Body," and fronts her interview podcast "Never Before" with *Lenny Letter*.

Janet lives in New York City with her husband, Aaron Tredwell. Find out more at JanetMock.com.

Read Janet Mock's first memoir,

Redefining Realness,

the profound and pioneering
New York Times bestseller

Pick up or download your copy today!